PIGSTICKING
A JOY FOR LIFE

William Rushton is the well-known television, radio and stage personality, illustrator, Daily Express columnist and Celebrity Square who recently extended his fame to the title of *Superpig* and who, with *Pigsticking – A Joy For Life*, hopes to have quelled some of his hitherto frustrations for something much dearer to his heart – his passion for sport.

Not perhaps the most athletic figure of a man in appearance, one should not be deceived – he is in fact a cricketer of renowned ability, can swing a golf club with surprising grace and elegance, is the proud winner of a Jack Nicklaus autographed putter, and knows his football and snooker backwards. He is also a sporting character of no meagre courage, having recently embarked on learning to swim, drive a car and shoot an arrow, among other foolhardy things, at a stage late enough in life to bring its own hazards as deterrents. He is now contemplating ballooning. . .

PIG-STICKING IS A ROUGH SPORT!

Also by William Rushton:

SUPER PIG

PIGSTICKING

WILLIAM RUSHTON

A JOY
FOR LIFE

A GENTLEMAN'S GUIDE TO SPORTING PASTIMES

ILLUSTRATED BY
WILLIAM RUSHTON

Futura Publications Limited
A Macdonald/Futura Book

A Macdonald/Futura Book

First published in 1977 by Macdonald & Jane's Limited.
This edition published by Macdonald & Jane's Publishers
in association with Futura Publications in 1978.

Designed by David Fordham

ISBN: 0 7088 1424 7

Printed in Great Britain by
Richard Clay (The Chaucer Press), Ltd.,
Bungay, Suffolk

Futura Publications Ltd,
110 Warner Road,
Camberwell, S.E.5

CONTENTS

AMATEUR CRAWLING

First and foremost I would like to award the dubious honour of Rushton's Sports Person of the Year to Suzi Ross Brown who, but for the laughably chauvinistic attitude of the Scots selectors, might well have been the first woman to set Murrayfield alight. She, it was, who, when unable to answer some of my more bizarre sporting queries from the deep recesses of her encyclopaedic mind would leave no divot unreplaced in her search for the solution. She is in fact another Leslie Welch – you may remember the Memory Man. (Raquel Welch, the Mammary Woman is no relation.) Magnificent Suzi, I hope your leg soon improves.

Secondly, I would like to thank *en masse* all those secretaries and the like of all the sporting bodies hereinafter mentioned, most of whom seem to be represented by the *Sports Council* and ensconced in *70 Brompton Road, London SW3*, a right House of Pleasure that must be. They were, *in toto*, a considerable help.

Peter O'Farrell, actor and chansonnier, a famous and fearful Royal Dwarf in his day, who helped fill the Horse Racing Section with jests and know-how, and another gentleman, who prefers to remain nameless, who revealed all about the danger of owning a racing horse. Dave Ismay, a comedian e'en now heading hot-foot for Baggy Nose Mountain, who kindly bequeathed me, prior to the bright lights, a number of the hoariest golfing stories available to golfing man

And how can I tastefully word my indebtedness to sultry, dynamic, ageing 24-year-old Rosalie Vicars-Harris who produced this book-like book from the rag-bag of ball-pointed hieroglyphs I presented her with? No way. David Fordham, who laid out the kicking beast, and somehow succeeded in making the drawings fit. Kate who typed it all out, and bought a house on the proceeds, and others that I have forgotten to mention, probably because they were no help whatsoever.

The author and publishers wish to thank the following individuals, picture libraries and organisations who kindly gave their help and, though not always possible to contact the original source, their permission to reproduce the following pictures in this book:

p. 10 Colorsport; p. 11 Barrie and Jenkins Ltd.; p. 21 *The Kill* by T. Rowlandson, Birmingham Museums and Art Gallery; p. 31 Fiona Vigors; p. 56 Moira Ryan Ainslie; p. 75 Granada Television; p. 92 Angling News Service Ltd.; p. 110 Art Seitz; p. 120 Goodchild's Ltd., The Adelphi; p. 128 Colorsport; p. 131 M.C.C., Lord's Cricket Ground; p. 133 Roger Kemp; p. 136 Basil Troth; p. 141 M.R.B. Way; p. 140 a postcard the author found in a drawer, undated, B.B. London Series (Germany); p. 165 Don Morley/All-Sport. Fishing tackle for the jacket photograph was kindly supplied by City Sportsman.

BREAKING IN

Should you detect at any moment in this book the whiff of sour grape-shot, I would like to point out that it is written by a man who has just entered his Roaring Forties and has never been asked to play for England at anything. And probably never will, I remember thinking, as I blew out the candles on the memorial cake, causing a conflagration such as there has not been since the local curry emporium laced my Vindaloo with gelignite after I dwelt too long on Tony Greig's trouncing of India. Were I to live my life again I wouldn't want to be Ombudsman, or on the board of I.C.I. or even have passed mathematics at 'O' Level. I would simply like to bat at Number 6 once or twice for England, go through Australia once perhaps with my telling lobs on a sticky wicket at Brisbane, save a penalty at Wembley, run a mile in under 20 minutes without being sick, sell a dummy to J. P. R. Williams at Cardiff Arms Park, and die happily at Alexandra Palace from a surfeit of Ruddles after winning the World's Darts Championship with two 'bulls' and a Double One. And not necessarily in that order, God, if you're listening. It's not a lot to ask really. 'But too late!' booms God, who has already pre-destined that when I do live my life again it will be as a bionic rabbit at the White City Greyhound Stadium.

Why have all my fantasies been sporting ones? Well, not all, admittedly, for there comes a time in every young lad's life when his fancy turns slightly. It was Ava Gardner who first burst into my reveries. I had Keith Miller in a number of minds as he threshed wildly at my high-tossed googly. The slow action replay, unavailable then (the nearest you got was a 78 of John Arlott played at $33\frac{1}{3}$), would have shown Miller paling visibly as he scythed to and fro in pursuit of my elusive delivery. It would also have shown the look of triumph on my finely-carved features turn to a look of total puzzlement as I asked myself the question – what on earth is Ava Gardner doing at the Nursery End? I admit I still pinned back her leg stump, and despite her and other ladies constant butting in – (I can recall lying on the centre-spot at Hampden Park while the England physiotherapist cleaned lipstick away from my damaged leg. She would chomp through shin-pads – Merle Oberon) – sport has always figured hugely in my wilder dreams.

And not just my dreams, I read newspapers from the back in the Chinese manner, spend Saturdays glued to *Grandstand* or *World of Sport*, and come to think of it, apart from odd games of cricket in the summer, very rarely stand up except for *Sportsnight with Fiona Richmond.*

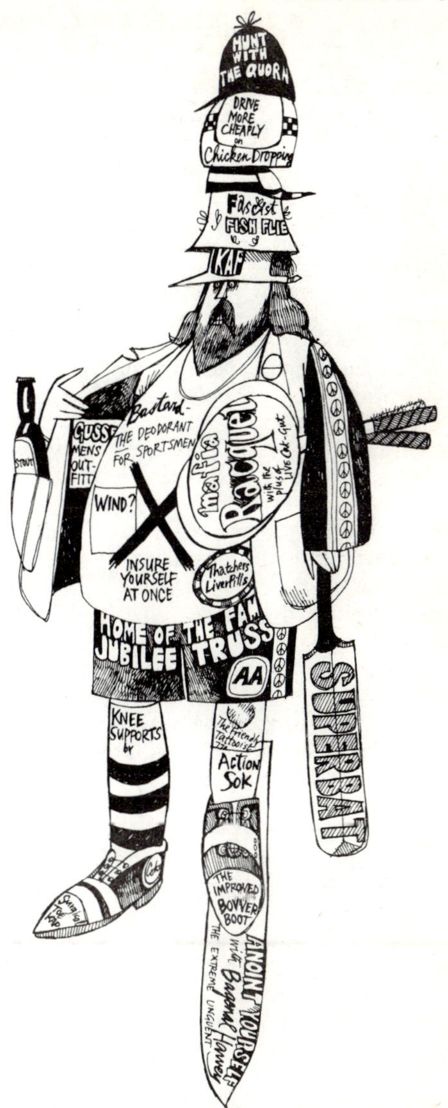

Not that sport is what it was. Most pleasures today are formed into limited companies or multinationals with creaking groaning boards and public relations officers, and are, like the rest of us, at the mercy of fluctuations of the market, bankruptcy, Swiss gnomes and Arab antics. Sport is now a serious business, like comedy, and yet it's fair to say that no one ever actually sat down and thought up a sport with the express idea of making money out of it. The number of games that emanated from monasteries demonstrate that. If you can imagine a wild whoop from the cloisters as Brother Bartholomew invented football and realised he was on to something vast financially, then how come the Venerable Bede never mentioned it? (*See 'Football'*)

For once you can't lay the blame entirely on the newspapers, though they may have contributed to the phasing-out of sheer enjoyment in sport. It's the telly, however, that has introduced the atmosphere of the operating theatre. There are times when watching some game of an afternoon on the box I feel like a young medical student attending a complex lobotomy conducted by a distinguished old surgeon with commentary provided. Having watched him saw the top off a head like a boiled egg from our seats in the gallery, and given him a warm round of applause, he then turns to us and announces that as there's not much going on in the skull at the moment, let us over to Sir Horace Walpole further down the body who's ready with a breath-taking vasectomy. Over now to this – over now to that – overmuch – overkill – over to Richie Benard at the end of the over. Action Replay – Action Foreplay – with the result at the end of it all we've watched the patient probed, dissected, dope-tested and analysed and sport lies bleeding.

And the newspapers have to shout louder to be heard. Ask for 'the Pink 'un' nowadays and you get *The Financial Times*. So whereas in days of yawn you could quietly clog an opponent of an afternoon, have a beer with him afterwards, and help him into the ambulance later, the best of friends, the incident now becomes a mini-Sarajevo.

In the same way that you curse a travel-writer in a glossy magazine who gives away your favourite watering-hole, so do you curse those who suddenly and violently popularise your personal pastime. 'Aha, but it's good for the sport!' they will say, belching cigar-smoke.

Dedication – to these Ladies – God Bless 'em.

It's only good for those who see the sport as something other than a pastime. For example, since *Pot Black* rocketed up the charts, try and find a friendly game of snooker. The tables are laden with Minnesota Fats. There are now professional darts players. Those friendly farmers who appear in *One Man and His Dog*, simple, decent men, whose only equipment to date is a crook and a sheepdog, will soon, God wot, be clad in tracksuits, their crooks stamped all over with the maker's name and their dogs trained to bark out in Morse the benefits of marrow-bone jelly.

The fun has gone out of it. Particularly for those of us in the Second XI of Life. Only there for the beer, and look what happened to skittles. They've become mechanised and computerised.

What I thought I'd do is amble through the corridors of sport and see if any joy can still be found there. There'll be moments of hope even as you pass the offices of the Don Revies or the Alec Bedsers. In the distance you will hear the cheery ululating of Eddie Waring or the refreshing noise of slap and tickle from George Best's boudoir.

If you look at sport you'll find, as you will find if you peruse the anatomy of Britain, its heart is in the right place, but the head is all to cock.

This book is therefore dedicated to my favourite team. The only one I know who simply enjoy what they do, and giggle and weep and whoop and laugh and cheer while at it. They come from a land not well-known for levity, and they play a game designed originally for obese businessmen, but they won a gold medal at Montreal and demonstrated totally that sport is not necessarily a preliminary to a Third World War, played in the spirit of the First World War. I love them madly – so hats off and shoes off too to the Japanese Ladies' Volleyball Team – a Bonsai Chorus Line.

Whatever happened to Saturday afternoon?

PIG-STICKING
IS A ROUGH SPORT.

PIG-STICKING OR HOG-HUNTING

A COMPLETE ACCOUNT FOR SPORTSMEN—
AND OTHERS

BY
SIR ROBERT BADEN-POWELL, BART.

A REVISED AND ENLARGED EDITION WITH FORTY-TWO NEW ILLUSTRATIONS DRAWN BY THE AUTHOR

"DUM SPIRO SPEARO"—*Old Shikari.*

HERBERT JENKINS LIMITED
3 YORK STREET · ST. JAMES'S
LONDON S.W.1 MCMXXIV

SKETCHED AT 9.15 A.M. ON 21ST OCTOBER, 1922.
(I don't say I saw it—I sketched it.)

A LITTLE UPSET.

A FOE WORTHY OF ONE'S STEEL.

PIG-STICKING – A JOY FOR LIFE

'Perhaps, excepting murder (ref., Genesis, Ch. 2) *pig-sticking is one of the oldest sports in the world.'*

SIR ROBERT BADEN-POWELL. BART.

This is the first sport I ever actually witnessed, and then it was a misprint.

At the beginning of the Second World War there was a deal of excitement in Newport, Monmouthshire, whither I had been evacuated, as a locally-barracked regiment of Indian cavalry were holding a gymkhana at the Rodney Parade, home of Newport's famed rugby side, the old black and ambers. It said on the posters there would be 'pig-sticking'. This transpired to be 'peg-sticking', another non-ball game entirely, but there was no Trades Description Act in those days, and entertainment was hard to come by, as were pigs if you think back, so no one complained. Pug-sticking is something else too, though still practised I believe in parts of Kensington, with umbrellas.

To relish the full flavour of this Cinderella of sports, I can heartily recommend *Pig-sticking or Hog-hunting, A Complete Account for Sportsmen – and Others* by Sir Robert Baden-Powell, Bart. (*try your library!*). In this most comprehensive work one runs the gamut of pigging. The history and nature of the sport, its value to the Indian Civil Service, the points of pig, the haunts of pig, the powers of pig, its speed, its cunning, its jinking, its ferocity, the author's failure to win the Kadir Cup – all are described in some detail.

The author tells how this 'manly and tip-top sport' came into being as a substitute for bear-sticking. Bear became scarce, so the bear-stickers took to pig and discovered that 'in the latter beast they had a foe more worthy of their steel'.

You need three riders armed with spears and a number of local inhabitants to beat the jungle and drive out the pig.

'When the boar is presently sighted', writes Sir Robert, 'and goes lobbing away at his stiff-looking canter, you all go crazy. You can't help it; horses and men, it's a mad race for all.'

The chase is on, the purpose of the game at this point is to get 'first spear' ahead of your team-mates. You get within range, 'and you turn your spear ready for use. It's like drawing swords in the gallop for the charge. It means suddenly business'.

Once stuck, of course, pig goes berserk and will charge at anything and anybody. And vice versa, until poor old pig is summoned to the great sty in the sky. Incidentally, only males may be wiped out, and certainly not sows or young 'squeakers'. In the Calcutta Tent Club (any taxi driver will tell you where it is) anyone

HOW TO STICK PIG
GB

found guilty of spearing a sow was fined a dozen bottles of champagne.

He quotes a veteran pig-sticker who charged with cruelty in his pursuit, retorted by instancing St George – the patron saint of cavalry – as a historical precedent.

There is more ripe old cobblers in this derelict old memoire of days now dead than will be found in five minutes by a fly on the wall of the boardroom of Sunday Bloody Sunday United, struggling though they be at the bottom of the Fourth Division under the weight of their 103-year-old mashed potato king chairman.

That's pig-sticking for you. What I can't discover is whether this Baden-Powell, who thought hog-hunting admirable because you mingle only with your own kind, and while the beaters, piggees etc. and others you wouldn't dream of inviting to tiffin grope about on foot in thick jungle, you and the lads are galloping free after the cheerful swine, is the same Baden-Powell who founded the Boy Scouts. If he is, I would suggest you hand in your woggle and garters. Not that he's made of stone, he points out that 'apart from the injustice of it, it's fatal to the interest of sport to ill-treat the villagers . . .' All too bloody true, what?

If you wish to contact Sir Robert his ghost, he maintains, can be reached at his sporting paradise 'Koila Gheel, Muttra'. He stayed there from 1882-1884 and bagged 428 pig.

Glossary of useless terms

Pig	*Soot, Bad, Dukar, Paddi, Kard Hundi, Cunijati, Banda*
Tushes	*Teeth*
Sounder	*Family of pig*
Pug	*Footprint of pig*
Puggee	*Tracker who follows footprints of pig*

YOU
and other PEOPLE'S
LEGS
CROFTAMIE G. Balding 9-10-5
PELHAM WOOD (6lb. ex.) Armytage
WATER COLOUR M. Tate 8-10-0
CURRENT MAGIC M. Tate 7-10-0 (C2)
Bewicke 8-10-0
MOSTLY MUSIC Mrs Evans 6-10-0
H. Evans
C. Smith 49
G. Jones 50
R. Hyett 45

MOST VIOLENT HORSEMANSHIP

HUNTING

'A good fox-hunter must possess in abundance those qualities which enable a man to manage a horse, to control a pack of hounds and to work successfully with his fellow men.' – Boring book published in 1941 when they should have been thinking of other things. The qualifications seem to let me out.

You could hunt. If you want to. I don't see why you should personally, or that you'll do anybody much good if you do, but if you must, you must. Perhaps you relish the taste of jugged fox, washed down with a cup of stirrup. Clearly the first prerequisite if you're absolutely determined to hunt is to be able to ride a horse. Actually, of course, this applies only to the hunting of foxes and the odd stag, poor sod, but if you like to see animals mangled by other animals then there are opportunities for pedestrians in beagling and the like. (*See Beagling and the like*)

It's no bad thing to be able to ride a horse. Particularly since given the activities of OPEC and the inactivities of British Rail and British Leyland, Britain will soon be back on its feet again, last legs, not to mention, knees. There are those who believe that if the car became extinct and we returned to horse transport where we belong, Britain would be a better place to live in. I can only recall my grandfather complaining that when a student at Bart's Hospital in the naughty nineties, the noise and smell of horse-drawn traffic was appalling. Traffic jams everywhere and the constant hazard of low-flying horse matter.

The advantages of riding a horse that I've had put to me are (*a*) the slowness in these giddy times and (*b*) the fact that you get a good view over other people's hedges. An acceptable form of prying as opposed to standing on the roof of the car, ostentatiously doing five miles per hour. There would always be someone behind you flashing headlights or hooting, there always is, but not if you're horse-borne. Cars fear horses. Fear of the sudden back-lash taking a headlamp or your A.A. badge. There is also the average punter's terror of a dead horse. Think of *The Godfather* or the terrible hush that falls over a racecourse when the vet moves in behind the screens.

Another advantage is that horses are relatively thick, compared with dogs for example. Have you ever tried to saddle a cat? This means they will do roughly what you tell them, even if they need constant reminding.

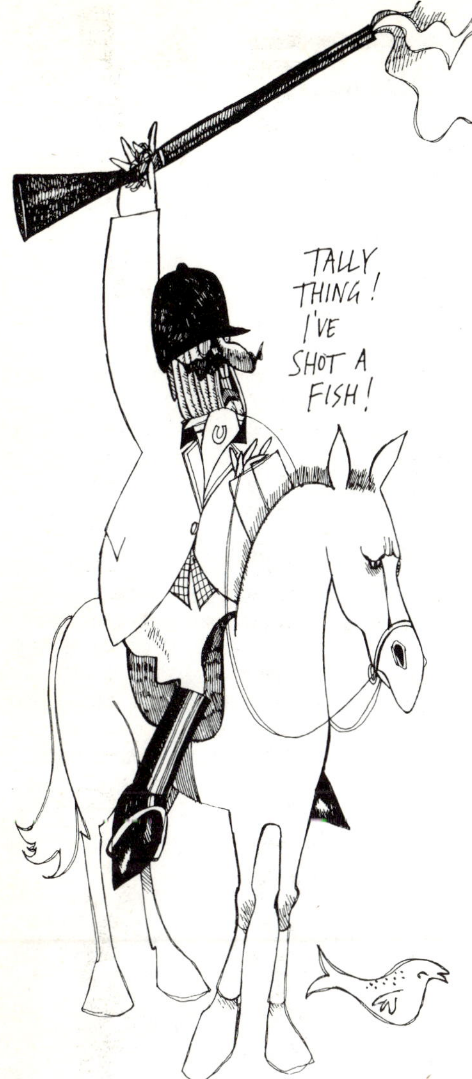

To Get You Mounted

You can get lessons in a class at a riding school (make sure it's not just 'licensed' but also 'approved') for about £1.50 an hour. If you're easily embarrassed and insist on private tuition this can cost you £4.50 an hour and could get extremely pricey as you have a long way to travel, bandy-legged and saddle-sore as you are – (I'd ride if horses were narrower).

You'll need a hard hat – £5 and upwards.

I'm reliably informed jodhpurs are the most comfortable trousering and weigh in at about £15 a pair. (John Wayne doesn't wear jodhpurs, a fact worth mentioning.)

Riding boots, and you might as well – £7 or more.

A tasteful jacket if you will – about £20.

Then there's the business of the beast. Pony prices are apparently determined by the price they'd fetch as meat. The Thelwell-type would clearly make good eating. *Vive la France!*

A kid's pony, ready to ride and raring to go will cost in the region of £90 and upwards and can be kitted out second-hand for about £30 (£40-ish if new). Indian tackle is, I gather, well-known for falling apart in the rain. Hence there's little racing there in the Monsoon Season.

If you're blessed with a field then you'll only have to feed the thing in winter on hay, of which, depending on winter's length and severity, you'll need about £35-worth. Cubes, about £50-worth per annum and oats will cost a further £30 or so.

In addition, of course, you will need the paraphernalia and trappings. Buckets, ropes, halters, hay-nets, rugs, grooming kit, etc. Not to mention the horse doctor who comes in at about £15 a visit, plus pills and medicaments and the burly blacksmith, with or without spreading chestnut tree (VAT incl.) who charges about £7 for a change of shoes. If you're field-less, housing the brute could set you back some £20 a week. And transport can prove quite dear. But you're determined. Very well.

Tally Ho, Angels One-Five, Roger and Out.

The British attitude to animals has always been written off as one of our eccentricities. It is however raving madness. Admittedly I am a city lad, born within the sound of Harrods, and although versed in London lore, a tracker's instinct for the nearest pub, a rare ability to dodge the ever-growing mounds of dog-shit while still apparently gazing aloft blinking at

ORIGINATORS & SOLE MAKERS

SPLIT-FALL OR FLY FRONT. **21/-** BUTTON OR LACED KNEES.

SEMI-RIDING KNICKERS.

Cut on the same lines as **Riding Breeches**—full on the Thigh—free from drag—very clean at the Knee—they will be found specially suitable for **Walking, Golfing, Fishing, Shooting, Riding, &c.**

MATERIALS.—Real Harris and Lewis Tweeds, Cottage, Mayo and Irish Homespuns, Donegal and Kenmare Tweeds, Shepherd's Checks, &c., &c.

FOR COLONIAL WEAR.—We recommend our celebrated **Triple-Yarn-Proofed Washing Garbette:** guaranteed thoroughly thorn-resisting and waterproofed.

A PERFECT FIT guaranteed by using our Simple Self-Measurement Form.

100 PATTERNS POST FREE on application.

Greatham, East Liss.

I am very pleased with the way in which my order was executed. The Cubbing Coat, Semi-riding Knickers and Gaiters fit splendidly. R. T. G. (Major).

REID BROS.

Sporting Tailors and Breeches Makers,

NORFOLK HOUSE, 209, Oxford St., LONDON, W.

Telegrams: "Tristan, London." Telephone: 8306 Gerrard.

From a Photograph.
Legging makers of every description.

the falling soot, I am as lost and confused in the country as a Cornishman on the Bakerloo. The Townie and the Countryman know different pleasures and should respect that, but you, sir, in the heavy tweeds and dungy boots, with the straw in your mouth, answer me this. If you can happily sally forth and blast away at venison with a 12-bore, why do you send your beef to the town abattoir when you could stick electrodes up them and have a fine day's sport shooting them as they leap and romp? They shoot horses don't they? You love to have dogs yapping at your heels and yet the fox, which is strangely similar, has its life made a misery and its death a pantomime version of the Trooping of the Colour. However, if I was to moot corgi-hunting as a viable alternative, I'd never dare show my face outside the walls of Kensington again. Not that you're entirely safe in here. My wife stood behind a gentleman in the Brompton Road Post Office while he renewed his hunting licence. God knows what he was after in these parts, but we haven't let the cat out since. Incidentally, we mouse together and have been known, in season, to rat.

The earliest form of hunting was clubbing stegosauri. It seems to have become less sporting since. The odds seem preferable in bull-fighting, particularly in Portugal where teams of Ports wrestle with the bull in extremely free style, like a team of circus clowns in a rugby scrum. Still I can't see members of the Quorn changing their ways at this late hour, at least not until one of their number is gored by a fox. I can assure them that bull-wrestling is a crowd-puller. Perhaps though they want to be alone.

Where To Flush Them Out

You can have the odd day's hunting with almost any pack in the country for as little as the price of a collection, or 'cap' as they call it as they pass it round. How much this is depends on the hunt but could be £20. There are only about three days in the year when you can actually latch yourself on to the regulars, unless you pay the full subscription – in England, for instance, £200 for South Notts, £120 in Ireland with the Limerick, and:

'If you hunt with the Duke of Buccleuch's
Up in Scotland they give you the works
Eighty quid in the box
Means a year chasing fox
Hence the phrase – a collection of burks.'

The season lasts from the end of the harvest when they're into 'cubbing' (which is instilling into the minds of young hounds the joys of beating up young cub foxes – this is what education is all about) and goes on until April.

The least I can do if you're absolutely adamant is point you to a book called *Baily's Hunting Directory* in which you will find details (gory and otherwise) of all the packs in Britain and Ireland and the money involved. Tell the truth, some are fairly tight-lipped about the

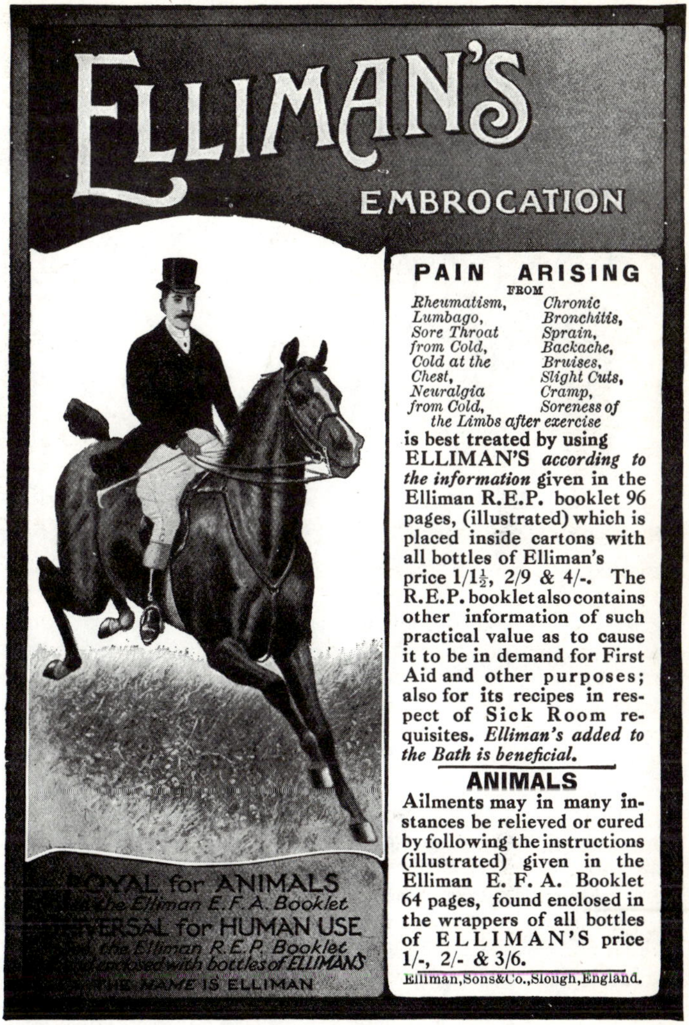

ELLIMAN'S EMBROCATION

PAIN ARISING FROM

Rheumatism, Lumbago, Sore Throat from Cold, Cold at the Chest, Neuralgia from Cold, Chronic Bronchitis, Sprain, Backache, Bruises, Slight Cuts, Cramp, Soreness of the Limbs after exercise

is best treated by using ELLIMAN'S *according to the information* given in the Elliman R.E.P. booklet 96 pages, (illustrated) which is placed inside cartons with all bottles of Elliman's price 1/1½, 2/9 & 4/-. The R.E.P. booklet also contains other information of such practical value as to cause it to be in demand for First Aid and other purposes; also for its recipes in respect of Sick Room requisites. *Elliman's added to the Bath is beneficial.*

ANIMALS

Ailments may in many instances be relieved or cured by following the instructions (illustrated) given in the Elliman E. F. A. Booklet 64 pages, found enclosed in the wrappers of all bottles of ELLIMAN'S price 1/-, 2/- & 3/6.

Elliman, Sons & Co., Slough, England.

OYAL for ANIMALS
the Elliman E.F.A. Booklet
VERSAL for HUMAN USE
the Elliman R.E.P. Booklet
enclosed with bottles of ELLIMAN'S
THE NAME IS ELLIMAN

money involved and merely say under Subscription 'Apply to Secretary'. The Secretary of the Duke of Beaufort's for instance said they never publish their subs, thus giving the impression that there's one sub for the rich and quite another for the Sheik of Araby.

Human Behaviour at the Hunt

You'll have spent about £75 kitting yourself out, and you'll be mounted on a feast of horsemeat, and you've paid your sub or whatever, so do try and get everything else right. A monster black for instance is 'heading' the fox. In case you think you've been accused of unnatural practice, what you have done is get in front of the fox and forced it to change direction. You will be made to feel a bit of a rotter.

And then there's the verbiage:

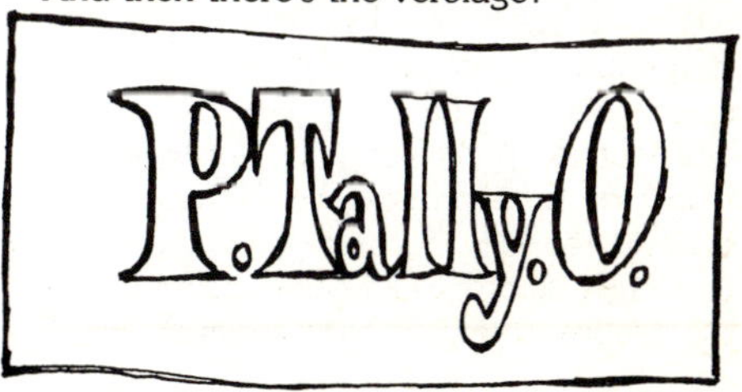

WRONG:	Where's everyone going?	RIGHT:	Hello, we're moving orf.
WRONG:	Nice lot of dogs.	RIGHT:	Fine pack of hounds.
WRONG:	32 of 'em, eh?	RIGHT:	16 couple, what?
WRONG:	They've smelt something, they're going woof! woof!	RIGHT:	They have picked up the scent and are giving tongue, speaking or giving voice.
WRONG:	The fox has pissed off.	RIGHT:	Gone away.
WRONG:	He's gone down a hole.	RIGHT:	He has gone to ground (in an earth).
WRONG:	Thar he blows! Fox!	RIGHT:	Aye! Aye! Charlie!
WRONG:	Eight o'clock right!	RIGHT:	(*or* Holler, spelt Holloa in hunting parlance, a strange sound – see Eddie Waring).
WRONG:	What's that in the red coat?	RIGHT:	That is the M.F.H. in pink. Named after a Mr Pink who initially ran them up.
WRONG:	Being M.F.H. must cost a bloody fortune?	RIGHT:	Right on baby.

NON-VIOLENT HORSEMANSHIP

DRESSAGE

Now whereas as a spectator my only views of hunting have been on gravy-stained table mats on the walls of some of our more pretentious pubs, (for example, a Rowlandson happily entitled *The Kill*, showing a joyful George IV waving his hat as a lot of dogs dismember a fox – which as a table mat encourages instant vegetarianism), I can watch the other horsey sports without a wince, indeed with pleasure. With the exception of dressage, which is boring as old boots, but then I don't like the horse turns at circuses.

I suppose dressage has never been popular enough to warrant their attention but otherwise it would have seemed a natural double-act for say Gene Kelly and Fred Astaire, housed in the same pantomime horse-skin, to have done a lively dance routine based on a dressage event. There is something of the soft-shoe shuffle about it, but not enough. Anyway there would have been quibbling over the billing, and intense argument over who played the back legs.

Even the Spanish Riding School leaves me stone cold dead in the market. Perhaps I only enjoy equestrian pastimes in which either the participants are in danger of falling off or you can put money on them.

SHOWING

Showing is another aspect of the business, but hardly comes under the heading of sport. As its name suggests all you do is show the animal. It therefore becomes an unexciting race between monied persons as to who can afford the best-looking beast. 'A very snooty lot', said a horsey person, and they know their snoot.

If you're only interested in looking at the shape of animals, their coiffure and make-up, then I recommend the Miss World Contest or Crufts. Dogs, after all, do fetch and sit, and come and go, and beg unaccompanied, so do Miss Worlds but with chaperones. Horses have to be encouraged with whips and crops. Not so dogs, possibly certain Miss Worlds.

I was upset recently, having long admired horses in their wild state to see a commercial on our television showing wonderful aerial views of a fine Black Beauty charging free over hill and dale, stream and beach, mane flowing, nostrils flaring, only to discover that the magnificent creature was seeking to open an account at Lloyds Bank.

EVENTING ONE'S BILE

The three-day event, as its name suggests, is designed for those who by a quirk of birth, an Act of God, have been blessed with, and view as their due, the long weekend. It is not a reference to Easter, however carefully phrased.

In fact, if you wish to event for Britain, it would be best to pack in any job you have and ride off into the sunset in search of a private income. It is not exactly a sport for all. It's not exactly a spectator sport either, as the cross-country section is extremely difficult to follow, five miles and 35-odd obstacles. Even on television they lose competitors for hours, and unless you get a mild thrill out of watching royalty fall into ponds, not much fun on the course. The first day is boring old dressage, and the third day, on which at least the points system becomes more rational and more easily followed, is Second XI show jumping.

Perhaps you think I'm trying to put you off the whole thing. I would only say this – the horse itself could cost you £5000 for starters, and they're not made of stone, you know, they come apart more easily than humans, particularly in a sport as hairy as eventing. And hairy it be, and you have to take your hat off to those who do it, some of them you are actually obliged to throw yourself bodily out of the way of, bowing and scraping as you go.

RUSHTON: 'Your Royal Highness?'

PRINCESS ANNE: 'You bearded twit!'

RUSHTON: 'Would you say Eventing was an elitist pastime?'

PRINCESS ANNE: 'God, you're stupid (cuffs passing child with rolled-up copy of the *Horse and Hound*). Of course it isn't. All one needs is a few acres in the country, paddocks and stabling, the odd groom and a string of horses. Would you mind licking one's boots, one dirtied them on an Expressman? One tells you, it's bloody hard work, and one has other duties to perform, like blanco-ing one's husband. Horses run in the family.'

RUSHTON: 'I know. I always expect your mother at the Trooping of the Colour to suddenly clear three serried ranks of the 1st Battalion, Coldstream Guards, scatter the orchestra, and set off home across Green Park at pace, hoofing pelicans to death with every stride.'

PRINCESS ANNE: EXPL*T*V* D*L*T*D

RUSHTON: 'William Rushton. News at Ten. Badminton.'

PRINCESS ANNE: 'Eventing, you bearded cretin!' (*Fade*)

SHOW JUMPING

Like three-day eventing, the British are rather good at this, in spite of the efforts of the British Powers That Be who forced a large number of our best to turn pro, Harvey Smith and David Broome to name but a huge few. The theory behind this was that we British (fair play, the game's the thing, it's not cricket, jolly sporting, the world admires a good loser, blast, we've lost again!) felt it was time to clear up the muddled business of 'shamateurism' in the equestrian sports. In eventing and dressage, of course, they don't need the money and in racing itself the issues are more clear-cut, but in show jumping, particularly when the telly seized upon it as a ratings-puller, and threw in David Vine and a hotted-up Mozart, it became less obvious who was doing what and for how much.

If, thought the British authorities, we muck *ourselves* out, then, as is ever the case, the world will follow our fine example. Thus purified and looking good, they waited for the world, shuffling uneasily as the Germans filled their jack-boots with gutteral laughter and the Italians roared into their vermicelli. And so it came to pass that we turned out the Twelfth Men in Montreal on horses they'd never met. Once again it was a lady jumper, sweet Debbie Johnsey who saved our purple face and further persuaded me that if I hear one more coy, chauvinistic reference to 'jockettes', (a coy, chauvinistic reference to lady jockeys and not a breed of ball-twisting underwear), from another racing commentator, I shall so place his microphone that the only sound emerging from him for the rest of his days will appear to be that of hippopotami rutting in a muddy water-hole. One place where woman has shown her equality, indeed on many occasions her superiority, is with a horse between her legs. But when you look at the brouhaha surrounding lady newsreaders or the first Sikh traffic wardenesses or Mother Thatcher you begin to wonder when man became such a silly bitch. Perhaps it's the fact the media pay more attention to firsts than lasts. For example, on the last day of the Roman Empire, the headlines would have read 'First Lady Gladiator comes Second'.

Show jumping is a cracking spectator sport, because you know what's going on all the time. You can see the poles flying, and there's a decent clock in the top right-hand corner. Some of the contests can whip you into a fine lather. I've been known to bite through the neck of a bottle during the puissance.

I imagine sponsorship is what caused the British voice of authority to have its attack, it's caused and causing conniptions all over the place, but if you can happily and without blushing name an event or race or competition after those who forked out the necessary, why on earth can't the competitors enter the ring mounted on 'Bognor Regis Building Society' or 'Treadwell Wall-To-Wall'. There might be occasion for complaint if Harvey

Smith rode in on 'Maltdrains Old and Nasty is the Beer to Make You Whistle', but Dorian Williams could handle it. He is extremely dexterous verbally. His patriotic fervour may go a little far at times, but I've heard him bewail our national weakness at the waterjump. We tend to fall down, or at least put a foot in the water. 'Oh, the British and water!' he will cry, and granite-like he who will not weep with him.

On the subject, however, of sponsorship, and it will rear again no doubt, television needs sport, sport needs television, both need money and the money needs both, and the Olympics needs all three.

How to be a show jumper and excite young girls at Wembley Baths

It all starts at the pony club. Frenzied mini-Shockemöhles on small, fat ponies belting over tiny obstacles, legs flapping, elbows akimbo, mothers screaming while Thelwell sketches and Shire-horsey ladies whinny and retired cavalry officers bellow like geldings fresh from James Herriot's teeth. Thence it's a long haul to Hickstead. In more ways than one as I discovered from an idle chat with Harvey Smith who while deadly on horseback and a pleasure to watch and indeed to drink with (hell to wrestle with, I would imagine),

seems to spend more time on the motorways of Europe, driving his enormous mobile home than actually engaged in jumping fences. I refrained from asking him what the correct procedure is if one of your horses falls out of an upper bunk on an autobahn.

To succeed you have to start young (goodbye, then). You must also possess a 'natural seat' and a wonderful sense of balance. (Several of those standing at the back have just fallen over.) It's expensive again, it costs from £1000 to £1500 per annum to keep a show jumper. That's more than a wife, but then, I suppose, it's probably larger. You will also need a keen sense of direction. My geographical bump is the envy of many, but I still marvel at the ease with which the jumpers find their way round, especially against the clock. I can only too plainly picture myself going backwards and forwards over the rustic gate searching vainly for the next left turn while hooters hoot and Raymond Brooks-Ward does his impersonation of Dorian Williams and vice versa. Bring up the Mozart, and exit left at gallop.

POLO

Good to watch, if you can find it, but you would be forced to mix with some very strange people – royalty, South Americans and a number of persons so English as to be unintelligible. Luther made much the same noise when trying to move his bowels during the Reformation. ('Luther?' they would enquire anxiously. 'No, tighter!' he would roar.) It's something, I would imagine, to do with constipation, cold lavatories and over-zealous nannies and nothing at all to do with polo except that it's a good place to listen to the frozen-jawed, high-pitched snorting of our upper class at play. It's also extremely difficult. Not only must you be good on a horse, but also be able to hit a moving ball from a moving horse with not much of an implement. Beginners practice on a wooden horse in a pit.

Lord Mountbatten told an interesting story to a gang of incredulous sporting personalities on one of those Grandstand's Television Sporting Person of the Year Award shows. It was of an extraordinary goal he once scored. The ball was propelled by another up the very arsehole of his horse, and all he had to do was ride through the goal and wait. I don't suppose that happens often, but apparently the game is action-packed and pacey. Spectators also get to participate. You are allowed to stamp down divots between chukkas. Pronounce this 'chukkas' with a long final syllable as in Lord Mountbatten's horse. Each last seven and a half minutes. You then change ponies like tennis players change rackets. As they cost an enormous sum and their upkeep and travelling expenses are relatively high – I'd forget it if I were you unless you're royal, South American or given to snorting.

THE SPORT OF QUEENS

'There is no place for republicanism in a country where the monarch and indeed her mother are fervent fans of the Turf and love a flutter like the rest of us punters. Anyway, who else would you put on the stamps or on the backs of threepenny bits? Hooray for the Jubilee!'

I SAID THAT *(TWICE IN 1977)*

'There's been an effing copedemic'

JULIAN WILSON *(ON THE BEEB HO HO HO)*

FLAT RACING

The problem here for you, if you want to become actively involved in flat racing is one of size. If you are petite, then you're in with a chance. Write to a trainer or more, extolling your tininess and your ability if you have it, to ride and, strangely, to box. The boxing is not absolutely essential, but it does help. There are annual finals held in London, and fearsome they are to watch, minute stable-lads going at each other like lunatic ferrets, but apparently a win for the stables is good for stable morale. Whether it's good for the lads is questionable, there is a brutish theory that boxing is good for boys, as it teaches them not to cry. I think this is a very British theory, my long-held belief is that, once you've learnt not to cry, you can also contain any urge to laugh, dance or shout with anger. You lose the ability to emote – hence, possibly, Lester Piggott, the mounted Buster Keaton. Richard Pitman on the other hand didn't box, 'too much of a coward', he says. Coward, I ask you? Perhaps he's punch-drunk.

Suffice to say, boxing prowess has been known to be sufficient grounds for being taken on, but in the main, they'll assess the size of your hands and feet, and judge your future stature from that. There are those lads, one

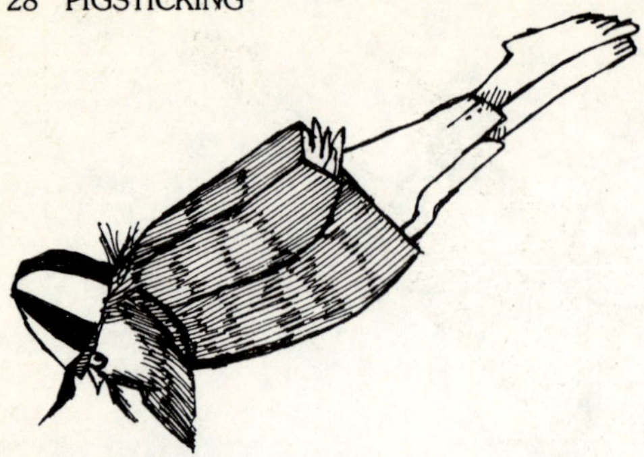

gathers, who have applied with their feet squeezed into boots sizes too small, but as those Chinese ladies found when after the Revolution their traditionally bandaged feet were loosed from bondage, the smaller they are the quicker you fall.

Given that you are too large, dare I suggest raising a son who could be a jockey? This could bring you joy as you watch the I.T.V. Seven in years to come. To guarantee this, and nothing is certain where breeding is concerned, you will need to marry, or certainly work your way round, a tiny woman. A tiny, horsey woman would be favourite, and worth a bob or two each way.

Discordant note

It was at this stage that the names, addresses and telephone numbers of a lively number of little and eminently suitable spinsters was to be inserted – but the printers have already made off with them. In their absence, I suggest you chance your arm with the Japanese Ladies' Volleyball Team.

Jockeys tend not to give birth to jockeys. Small men tend to fancy enormous women. There is the story of the circus midget who married the fat lady, and all that the crowd could hear from within the caravan, as they packed about it on the wedding night was the pitter-pat of the diminutive spouse crying 'Acres and acres of it, and all mine!'. They are also given to invading Poland.

Who to write to

You'll find the names and addresses of trainers in the *Sporting Chronicle's Horses in Training* – published every March.

Or you could be accepted for an Apprentice Training Scheme by applying to Brigadier Henry Green at *the Jockey Club, 42 Portman Square, London, W.1*. Few get in direct though, the majority are entered by trainers.

Owning a Leg or Two

This is perhaps your best entrée into racing circles. After all the life of a jockey is tough as underdone *Cheval Diane* with tired chips.

There was this morning-fresh, pristine Presbyterian Scot who drifted south, innocent as a lamb, and was depraved and corrupted, and instantly converted to a life dedicated to the Turf at the first meeting he ever attended, when by happy chance he won £190 for a 10-shilling Yankee. The next day he brought off an £80 Treble. He immediately thought racing was the simple route to the Cayman Islands, and set about finding 11 others eager as he to form a syndicate, (12 is the maximum ordained by the Jockey Club – though illegal as it is, you can share your leg so to speak) and share with him the appalling burden of vast wealth. Armed with their accumulated funds, he approached a friendly bloodstock agent, retraced a few steps on hearing that

gentleman had only that minute snapped up something of a gift-horse for Lady Beaverbrook for only £110,000, but recovered sufficiently to press £600 (£50 each they'd mustered) into his silvery palm.

Bargains are available. By about 1.30 p.m. in Dublin the Ring is apparently stiff with limping, vomiting customers, their judgement blown, and the auctioneer is thirsting for his lunch. A horse was purchased for £200, the cheapest in training that year.

It ran 10 times – four firsts, three seconds, and three thirds, amounting to £4000 in prize money. They were offered £12,000 for the animal, turned it down, and sold it the next year for £4000.

Not such a cheery syndicate, however, was one run Mafia-style by a dentist. The trainer is now awaiting Her Majesty's pleasure in some penal institution. (You will immediately point out that as her Majesty's pleasure is racing, he must be on to a good thing.)

Eight hundred pounds this horse cost the syndicate, though as they discovered later it only set the trainer back £400. Anyway, they never saw it, it trained for seven months, but never actually showed its face in public. 'Don't rush it', said the trainer. 'Grand National prospect', and probably tapped the side of his nose. Another month passed, and the syndicate began to wonder idly if there was a horse at all. The trainer finally caved in. 'O.K., I'll run it at an evening meeting at Sedgefield.' The syndicate gathered for the approaching triumph. It was in the last race at 8.45 p.m. Luckily the colours they had chosen were that luminous orange favoured by lollipop-men and traffic wardens, so that at 9.5 p.m. they could quite easily detect amidst th'encircling gloom the distant pin-point of light as their jockey slowly led the beast home.

The syndicate was slightly put out. 'I told you so', said the trainer. 'I told you it needed time.' Few can argue with trainers, like lawyers

and doctors, they are surrounded by high walls, padded with bull's excrement.

Even the wealthiest of owners can be deceived. Rolling up to view their new £70,000 colt they are unaware that the creature has been freshly greased to make the coat glisten. 'Doesn't he look well?' enquires the trainer, a favourite phrase and cigars bob in happy agreement.

Our syndicate's next excitement was in the middle of a week at Newbury. They couldn't actually be there to enjoy, and this in fact, the trainer knew. He also knew that they would all excuse themselves at the witching hour and disappear into a betting shop to listen to the race. The trainer took the jockey in a vice-like grip. 'The daft sods will be all ears', he said. 'Get to the first hurdle first whatever. Ride like Jehu from the start. This will make our owners strangely content.'

And how happy they were to hear their animal four lengths ahead at the first obstacle. It led for the first half-mile, mainly because no other jockey cared to pursue it, realising that Mother Nature was bound to intervene. Mother Nature certainly did and some distance short of the finish, the horse slowed to a grinding halt.

'You wouldn't believe it', said the trainer later, employing another favourite phrase of his breed, 'You wouldn't credit it. A young lad was playing with a kite. The kite broke loose. I see your jaws dangling is disbelief. The string, is fact not so much stranger than fiction, lads, the string wrapped itself round our horse's head and our jockey was obliged to dismount and undo it. Even so –', he paused, and plucked yet another old favourite from the air, 'it finished like a train'.

Four weeks later he was on the telephone.

'I'm afraid there's been an accident', he reported. 'Your horse broke loose in training, shed its jockey, and headed for the end of the field. I've never seen a hedge that size cleared with such ease. It's a good foot and a half higher than Becher's. Ah!' he sighed deeply, 'what a National prospect it was'.

'*Was?*' cried the syndicate.

'On the other side of that hedge', continued the harrowed trainer, 'lies the A4, and off down it, sirs, went your horse, overtaking the traffic, would you believe, on the outside lane. It would have won the 1963 Derby at that pace. A police car couldn't catch it. Finally, it came to a roundabout under repair, and charging bravely straight across it, impaled itself on a temporary railing.' He removed his tiny trilby, a rare spectacle. The syndicate lifted their flagging spirits manfully. 'What about the insurance?' they cried, as one. All was not lost.

'By chance, sirs', said the trainer, 'a Harley

Street vet was passing at the time and performed an emergency two-hour operation, opening the horse's chest on that very roundabout and removing the railing. The lucky creature, I am happy to report, lives, but will never race again.'

'Bastardy!' said the syndicate, unfeelingly.

Other favourite phrases to cause suspicion in owner's mind:

'Stone-cold certainty', 'Will piss in', 'Will win five minutes'.

The point about horses is that there's no telling what they'll do, which is why bookmakers are invariably such a happy breed. They can simply hate their fellow-creatures, or be incurably lazy. Horses, that is; and some bookmakers.

A first-class trainer will charge you about £50 a week for all his services, which isn't bad split between 12 of you if 12 there be. A slightly lesser man, and none the worse for that, (one such had 47 winners in 1976) will charge £30-£35. It seems to be cheaper in the North.

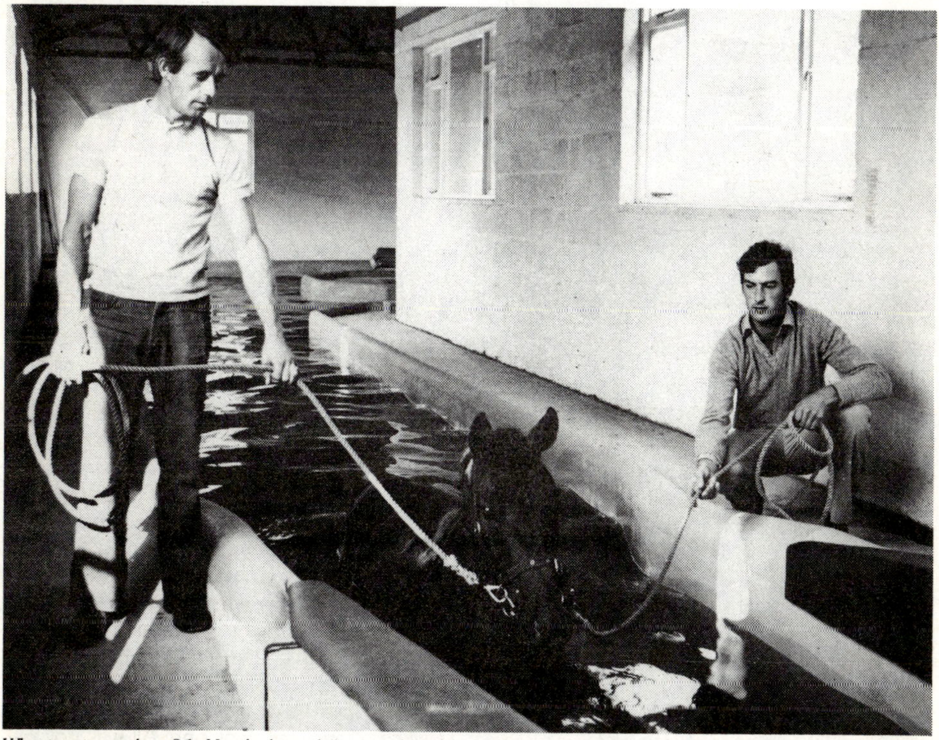

What is going on here? **1.** *Has the horse fallen in a sheep-dip?* **2.** *Is the beast being trained for water polo or the Venetian Grand National?* **3.** *Or coached to sprint in extremely heavy going at Uttoxeter?*

STEEPLECHASING

It's never too old to take this up. Look at the Duke of Albuquerque. Whoops, there he goes again! Now to my mind steeplechasing is more like it. It's more true to life than the Flat. Not my life, not my Flat either, but their life, the blissful union of man and horse. It strikes me at a safe distance as more natural for the pair of them to be bounding over hedges and stagnant water, up to their hocks in mud as they vanish into the distant fog at Chepstow, than belting up five furlongs of firm Flat.

There's something about starting stalls for instance that smacks a trifle of the plasticated bowling alley. They probably make life simpler for the starter (that seems a good job to pursue, reader, particularly if you are an ex-Colonel with no one left otherwise to shout at. Golf club secretary is another possibility if you're of that breed). I can remember seeing the inaptly-named jockey, R. Still, soaring vertically from the saddle like a Hawker Harrier as the old wires seized him at Alexandra Park that was. But compare the stalls-start with the wild charge at the beginning of the Grand National, for instance, and it's no contest.

Alexandra Park, now there was a race-course, nestling under the majestic birthplace of British Television. It was a grand spot for Londoners of a summer's day. Everything about it was in miniature, the jockeys seemed giants in comparison. The start was by the mini Members' Enclosure, as was the finish. The race would set off downhill for a couple of furlongs and that was the last you would see of it, as they then made up the necessary distances round and round a figure of eight, lost to view before setting off back uphill again for the final two furlongs. The commentator would give the impression he was following their activities, but I always imagined the lads were sitting quietly playing cards or passing the hip-flask, prior to organising a rousing climax. It is typical of progress that the course is now no more.

The hairiest of all steeplechases, apart from the National, is the Pardubice Steeplechase in Czechoslovakia. As Siena is to the Flat, and wouldn't it be fun to have racing again in the middle of London, (Leicester Square for instance), so is Pardubice to the chase. To watch it is to be at the last charge of Polish Lancers against German machine-guns. The hedges are enormous, the water wide and deep, at every jump a dozen horses fall as if dead, jockeys apparently drowned are artificially respirated, thrown back on their mounts, spitting tadpoles, and off they go again. It was won a few years ago by an Englishman, Chris Collins, and I've never been able to understand why he wasn't knighted. He stands with Sir Edmund Hillary and Sir Francis Chichester, great lunatics of the old school.

THE WAY TO AINTREE

If you are determinedly set on Aintree you'll have to work your way up from *point-to-points*. At these amateurs race round fields full of Range Rovers, belching port. Organised in the main by local hunts, your horse will have to have hunted on a given number of occasions to qualify. Originally, as its name implies, it was literally from point to point, as indeed was steeplechasing a chase to the nearest steeple, and the last one there's a poltroon or such.

The main disadvantage of seeking advancement in this particular sport is the appalling danger. Few top steeplechasers are not held together by wire, screws, pins and surgical sellotape.

Nonetheless a grand sport for the spectator, and invariably better odds for the amateur punter. The highest praise I can allow it is that you can watch a steeplechase spellbound and cheering without having a bet on a thing in it.

AMATEUR PUNTING

The truly amateur punter is he who studiously avoids backing favourites as the return is so pathetic and the excitement minimal. Instead he invests in 16-1 shots or more for no better reason than that the horse's name makes him laugh, the colours or the jockey remind him of a distant mother, or the creature has not been deemed worthy of mention by any newspaper tipster, and appears on the charts as 'Bar One'. We are the bookies' friend.

If you're at the course and have a firm fancy, your mother appears to be riding a long-shot named after your bank manager, shop around the bookies. Some will quote your choice at 33-1 say, others, 50-1 or 25-1, there will be those who haven't even deigned to waste chalk on it. Ask. Naturally, they will scoff, but, oh, the rare delight if it storms home triumphant. And even if it doesn't, don't petulantly rip up your betting slip until the tannoy rasps 'Weighed in'. The amateur punter must ever live in hope. It is not unknown for the first three to be disqualified. We're looking for Eldorado, not Hoddesden.

For more complex betting, dual forecasts and daily doubles, go to the Tote, you can be less efficient there, friendly ladies will explain all. Ooze charm and money through the tiny window, and they are yours.

I am in the main a Saturday afternoon telly punter. Bringing off the I.T.V. Seven is one dream, the B.B.C. Triella another – but I would recommend a gentle Yankee. This is not a literary reference to the Quiet American, but a simple bet that can feather your cap. Pick four horses in four different races, go to the betting shop and carefully inscribe '10p Win Yankee' at the top ot the slip and the names of your four. As you have 11 bets going for you in a Yankee, six doubles, four trebles, and one accumulator, multiply your stake unit by 11, in this case it comes to £1.10, and slap slip and money over the counter.

If your four nags are at good, healthy long odds make it a 10p Each Way Yankee, and multiply by 22. If all four come up, Happy Christmas! If three come up, you're still laughing as you have three doubles and a treble working for you, and if two win you still have a double (they can be rewarding – the winnings and stake money from win one are multiplied by the odds on win two – it beats backing them separately). One moment of truth is when the first three of your four have all failed you and your Yankee is over. I have found there is a tendency for horse four, knowing you have lost all interest in it, to win. Do not hesitate to lope across to the shop and frustrate the creature's basic meanness. For the more ambitious there is the Canadian (same principle but five selections giving you 26 bets, so a 10p Win Canadian is equal to £2.60). Or the Heinz, which is six selections giving you, ho, ho, ho, 57 bets, 15 doubles, 20 trebles, 15-4-selection accumulators, 6-5-selection accumulators and 1-6-selection accumulator. Ten pence Win Heinz is equal to £5.70. What a jolly Saturday afternoon.

My attitude to punting in particular and racing in general was coloured some years ago at Randwick Races in Sydney, Australia. I saw a person put $4000 on a horse to win $1000. It was certain, cast-iron, the new superhorse, fresh from 12 victories on the trot, and it came ninth. Of course, racing is honest as Robin Day is long. The late Duke of Norfolk espied a trainer slipping his horse a lump of sugar prior to the big race. 'My apologies, Your Grace', the trainer mumbled, knuckling his forelock the while, 'but he has a sweet tooth and who am I to deny the beast a little pleasure. Have

one yourself'. Together, the Duke, the trainer and the horse chomped on their lumps. The Duke made off, seemingly satisfied that all was above board. The trainer seized the jockey and said, 'Five furlongs out I want you laying about fifth – three furlongs out third – start kicking about one and a half out and at the furlong pole give him some stick, stay at him till the post – and don't panic if anything passes you, it's either me or the Duke'.

Studying Form

An evening paper (lunchtime edition) will give you all the tipsters' tips. The *Morning Star* has the wilder suggestions usually. Con the race in the paper.

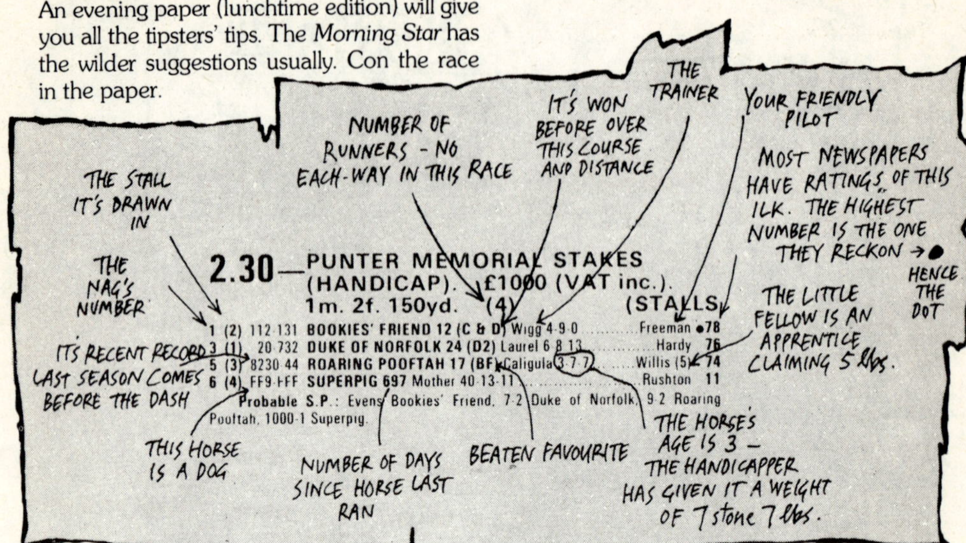

Punting Parlance

Age *In a horse it's worked out from 1 January of each year, regardless of its birthday.*

Aged *Over six years old, poor senile animal.*

Airing *Horse in a race for the exercise, not the money.*

Amiss *Filly or mare 'in season', tend to run below par.*

Ante-post *Betting before the day of the race. Odds are normally better, but you lose bets on non-runners.*

Bar *Not bookie using old-world expletive. But as in '2-1 the Field! 8-1 Bar!' The Field – favourite or co-favourites are at 2-1, but there are horses available at longer odds. Yours, presumably.*

Blinkers *Quite attractive to the amateur punter when worn for the first time. They promise miracles.*

Bumper *An amateur rider.*

Chalk jockey *One not experienced enough to have his name printed in permanent letters on the number board.*

Dog *A non-trier.*

Dwelt *Slow at the start. Mine tend to dwell.*

Enquiry *A moment of hope quite often for the amateur punter.*

Gelding *Snip, Snip, and Bob's your auntie.*

Genuine *A trier.*

Grand *£1000.*

Horse *A male thoroughbred of five or over, untouched by human scissors.*

Let down *A jockey does this riding his horse hard for the post.*

Lie up *A horse is doing this when racing.*

Maiden *A unisex term for a horse that hasn't won yet.*

Monkey *£500.*

Nursery *Handicap for two-year-olds only.*

Objection *Further hope for the amateur punter or a coronary.*

Overweight *Weights are put in the saddle to bring a jockey up to the weight allocated by the handicapper. At Kempton once a 4 stone 8 pounds boy rode at 10 stone 6 pounds and won. It took him an hour to carry the saddle from the Unsaddling Enclosure to the Clerk of the Scales.*

Out of *His father and mother.*

Over the top *A horse who's been over-raced or is bored.*

Pony *£25.*

Stayer *A horse that comes into its own after a mile and a half or more.*

Thief *Another dog.*

Triple Crown *The Derby, 2000 Guineas and the St Leger.*

Under starter's orders *The white flag's up they're well-nigh off. All bets stand.*

Weigh-in *After the race, the winner has his weight checked.*

OTHER BEASTS TO BURDEN

PIGEON FANCYING

You may be feeling a little low and dispirited, and I feel it's my fault. I've probably put you off becoming an international polo player. I haven't really tried to persuade you to hunt either, not that you *can* hunt for England. You can jump for England though if you go for your life, starting now.

Before you go though, how about pigeon fancying for your country? 'My dad fancies pigeons for Britain.' It has a ring, and although a similar incident is recorded in the Manual of Military Law, which is well worth a read I promise you, as a sport it has advantages.

Again initially it's not a cheap pursuit. You'll need a loft, out in the garden or on the roof or wherever, one large enough to hold 15 pairs of birds. The nest-boxes, perches, etc., about 10 ft by 6 ft, will cost you around £200.

You'll need a timer clock if you're going to race your birds, and you must. The cheapest new one listed is £75, but you can get them second-hand.

The actual birds are the least of your problems. Peruse the 'Fancy Press'. You've rather foolishly purchased *Gay News*. The 'Fancy Press' is a happy nomer for the *British Homing World* and *The Racing Pigeon*, both weekly and required reading for man and bird alike.

A reasonable bird can cost as little as £3. Admittedly at the other end of the perch there are those that fetch £5000. Start small however (a young pigeon incidentally is called a squeaker), not so small though as to accept a free bird from a fellow fancier . . . I think I'll start this sentence again, it's open to alarming triple *entendre* . . . not so small as to accept a

free *pigeon* from a fellow *pigeon* fancier. The knowledgeable point out that if you get a pigeon for nothing, there must be something wrong with it.

A pigeon is a good cheap thing to run. An ounce a day of pigeon corn in the racing season, and a dash more in the breeding season. Breeding tells. (Pigeons are monogamous as I recall, which is rather touching, as they all look the same to me.) Pigeon corn costs about £8 per cwt, so the honest bird sets you back about ½p a day – which 25 years ago, of course, would have bought you an Oxo cube, a free run of the conveniences or a whistle. How times have changed.

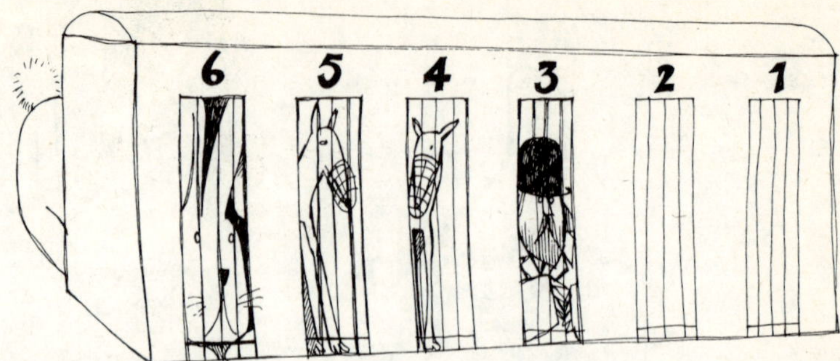

Getting the Bird Aloft or Ex-loft

Join a club (50p or so). This way not only do you get in with the old hands, and learn in a flash the secrets of choosing, breeding and training, etc., but you also get cheap transportation. A large lorry, is provided to get your birds to the various race points. This is where your timer clock comes into play. The club set it the evening before the race and seal it. At the end of the race as your pigeon triumphantly returns to the fold or loft, you stick its leg ring into the clock and record its time over the distance, or toss, as they know it in fancy circles, and they do get about. Advise the bird to avoid flying over Italy as they blaze away ruthlessly at anything that flaps.

Apart from the racing, there are also olympiads held by the International Federation every two years. There are two types of competition in these; one based on each country's team results and the other on conformation, a more tasteful word for beauty contest than anything Eric Morley has come up with.

GREYHOUND RACING

'The Dogs' as they're known – as opposed to hounds. This is a possible alternative for those who see themselves as owners. It's cheaper than the parts of a racehorse, though possibly not such good eating. You can actually go the whole dog quite reasonably.

You can get a dog for any price from £20 to £1000 upwards at one of the public auctions run at a track. Hackney, for instance, hold one monthly. Or get in touch with the racing manager at your local stadium and ask him to advise you on a dog or a trainer. This could cost you £150 or £200 straight up but you're less likely to wind up with a dog in a manger. For example, the bottom for a dog is to become a 'registered wide runner'. If you buy one there's a wonderfully precise and detailed registration form to be filled in mapping and detailing every inch of the dog, down to the exact colour of the toe-nails.

There are those who will train the dog themselves at home, bearing all the expense of kennelling and feeding, and the hideous business of walking the animal for miles daily. In Sydney I knew cat-owners who lived in constant fear of the passing do-it-yourself trainer, as a good cat, claws and teeth removed, provided a lively substitute for the electric hare. This would, of course, never happen here. (Exits left to check on whereabouts of scrofulous tom moggy.)

All this can be avoided by putting the dog in kennels where they are expertly fed and trained for you for £10 to £20 a week. The trainer rings you up and says, 'you're racing at the White City Stadium Thursday', and off you go for a merry evening's owning. I'm very partial to an evening at the Dogs, it's akin to roulette, but sportier. You can take a party, sit down to a large meal, and watch the dogs

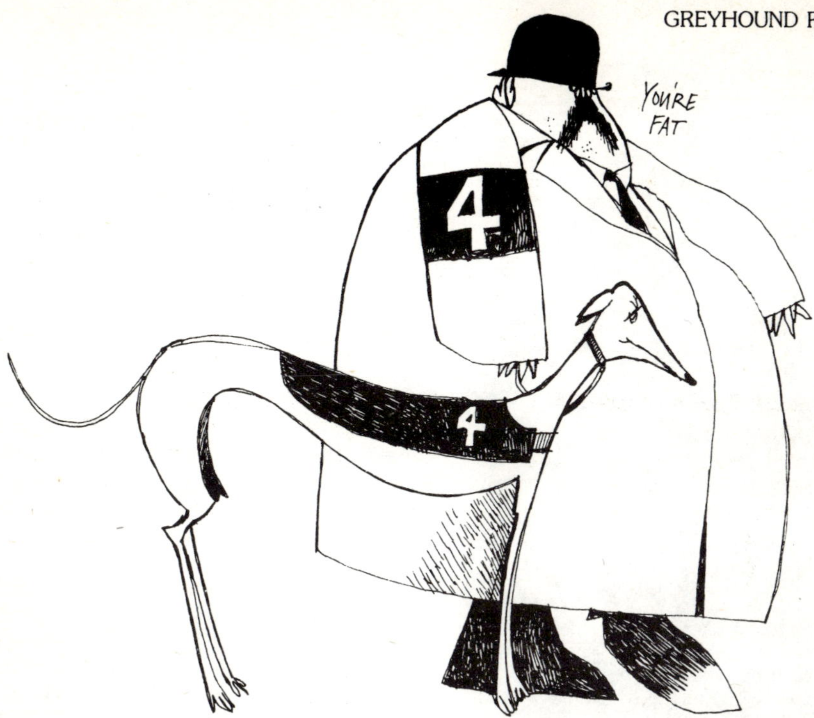

belt past the window while gracious ladies hover at your elbow to place your bets. It's something akin to Paradise.

There are basically two types of race. Graded races for dogs attached to that particular track, and hopefully matched by the racing manager to produce a massive dead-heat. Or Open Races. They hurdle as well. There are few finer spectacles than a slow-motion replay of a dog falling at a hurdle.

A Mild Flutter

Not that mild, in fact, at the Dogs, as the races are only 20 minutes apart, and by the time you've picked up your winnings, decided on your next bet and laid it, you're off again at a wild gallop to try and catch the end of the race.

I will admit I never look at the Form at all, this saves brain damage. I do precisely the same bet every race regardless and always have. It's a Three-Dog Combination Forecast, which covers half the field after all, and means that if any two of your three come first and second, you've pulled off a winning forecast, which can show quite healthy dividends. My three have always been Dogs One, Five and Six. I still find it remarkable how often Dogs Two, Three and Four come roaring in. Simply ask at the Tote for a Three-Dog Combination Forecast and give your three numbers. If it's a 50p Combination Forecast multiply by six and give them £3, a 20p Combination Forecast, obviously £1.20.

At the betting shop simply inscribe '50p C/Fcst.', the race and whereabouts, any three numbers from one to six and write boldly total stake – '£3'.

My only added extravagance on occasion is picking out one of the more generous-looking bookmakers and implanting a falling pound on the rank outsider. Again they scoff a lot, but if one 22-1 shot lopes home, watch the thinning of the lip and hoot.

My most uplifting moment was in Sydney again, where they have eight-dog races – (and of course eight-ball overs, discuss this oddity, answers on a plain postcard to this address) – which meant a change in a lifetime's habit. So Dogs One, Five and dear old Six gave way to One, Four and Eight and with no success whatsoever for the first seven races. However in the last race when One, Four and Eight seemed to figure in no-one's prophecies, I persevered with the faithless hounds. One and Four obliged and for an outlay of two shillings I became the proud possessor of some £80 Australian. My word, I've lived.

The author's wife riding an elephant along a beach somewhere north of Sydney, Australia. It is not a popular mode of transport in those parts, especially with picnickers. Nor is there any racing.

ELEPHANT RACING

I have some rather unsettling news on this score. Eight years ago or so, on my way to the Antipodes, I stayed a night or two in Colombo in Ceylon as it then was. Much to my chagrin I discovered that I had missed the Elephant Races, slated for May that year, by about three months. To compensate for this, I thought how good to throw it in here as a possible for you in your search for something small you can call your own. However, requests put to the now Sri-Lanka Embassy for information about the sport, opportunities therein for British mahouts and perhaps photographs of previous Derbies for the non-believers, were met with an agitated 'No way. Never. Elephant racing? Don't be daft. Not at all. Ever. Good day!'

I'm glad of the chance to reveal this to a startled world, but at the same time shocked and sorry nonetheless. I must write to Marjorie Proops.

CAMEL RIDING

Not a lot of it here, but if you grab 14 days in North Africa you can get some in. We used to have a Camel Corps, but that went in some defence cuts, otherwise you could at least have ridden for the Regiment.

I once set Shirley Maclaine on the roar, (I throw her name in casually, mainly to glamourise the index), with the tale of my only camel ride. Pissed as a judge having lunched over well near the Pyramids, I was inveigled by a cheerful Son of Araby onto the back of his camel. He insisted on wearing my dapper trilby and I wore his more exotic knotted handkerchief. Having established, as we rounded the Great Pyramid for the third time at a queasy lurch that I was in the acting business, he asked if I knew Jack Hulbert. 'Of him', I shouted back down from my hump. 'I was in *The Camels Are Coming*', he called back. He made it sound like David Attenborough's first blue movie, but I remembered seeing it years ago, and in no time, he, scuttering along the sand, and I, swaying above him, were joined in song.

'Who's been polishing up the sun?
Trying to make the moon shine brighter?'

As an incident, it has rarity value. The Sphinx laughed, and a week or two later the Six Day's War started. It may not have been sport exactly, but it was international.

YOU
and the
Machine
SUPER SWILL
28
28
28

WHERE THERE'S A WHEEL . . .

There is such a variety of machine sports that if you really can't stand dogs, are allergic to horse-hair in the home, refuse to stick pigs despite my urging, then pursue one.

Quite frankly under this heading I would include pinball (Gottlieb or Williams are the names to look for); those wondrous tennis games you can have attached to your television, known in America as pong games, which apparently leave irreparable tracks across your screen, but what the hell; bar billiards; and hoovering. All fine activities for brain and muscle but as yet unrecognised internationally, and it's the Red Rose on your pyjamas we're fighting for.

So, among others, we're going to look at cycles, the motor car and the aeroplane. All machines in which it is possible to make your mark for Queen and country, even if you're finally reduced to bombing Dresden again.

KARTING

No mean alternative to the other forms of motor sport. Karts are extremely simple to drive, not unlike souped-up super-dodgems in practice. The push-start sounds hazardous – belting after the tiny beast and leaping in when the engine starts, I would have thought it was very easy to miss. You can reach speeds of up to 80 m.p.h. on the straight, but as you're squatting hunched on very little and so close to the ground, it feels more like 180 m.p.h. A 250 c.c. kart can reach speeds of 150 m.p.h. I think you just lost me.

A chassis will cost you £150 for a second-hand job, or £275 new. The engine, second-hand £150, and new upwards of £200. As in all motor sport it pays to be mechanical, and much of the pleasure of karting is tinkering with the machinery. You get plenty of opportunities as, for instance, apart from the old crafts like tuning, you need different sprockets for different tracks and as each sprocket costs about £3 and may have sets ranging from 44 to 80, it can get expensive, even when it's do-it-yourself. A basic tool-set costs £30 at least. In a bad year it could cost you £1000 to race.

There are about 40 tracks in the country, all private, and provided you're insured, and over 12, you're off. You pay by the hour for the use of the track, and it works out considerably cheaper than a few minutes at 20 miles an hour on a tiny circuit at a fairground. A club sub will be about a fiver and a practice

session £1.50 or so. When you think you've practiced sufficiently you can apply to the R.A.C. for a competition licence. The wonderful aspect of it all is that you need never have driven a car in your life. This does not apply to Formula One for instance.

They maintain that karting provides all the thrills and spills of Formula One Grand Prix racing at prices you may be able to afford. As they say, 'In the *mêlée* of a kart meeting, drivers frequently run over each other; barge each other's rear ends as a recognised tactic; and use such terms as "shutting the door" for an exercise which involves the high-speed baulking of a rival's overtaking attempt'.

All human life is there and James Hunt is a cissy.

MOTOR RACING

My involvement with Grand Prix motor racing was brief but extremely comfortable. In the spring of 1974 I was summoned to Silverstone by the Lord Hesketh, to study the sport and write a piece about it for the glossy souvenir book he planned to sell at Brands Hatch later in the year when the British Grand Prix was on. Silverstone was a warm-up for the season and, indeed, a warm-up for me as until that day I'd believed Formula One to be an intravenal pick-me-up for those over-40s whose sex-drive was in reverse.

Now motor racing like so many other sports – swimming the 5000 metres, Olympic walking – bears no, absolutely no relation to its lay counterpart. Any resemblance between an Olympic walker and any other pedestrian is fictitious. They bear no relation to any person, living or dead, particularly walking. There are those who believe that the living dead walk, (*see Zombies*) but no one walks like an Olympic walker.

In the same way, motor racing has little to do with driving. Admittedly they travel at enormous pace, in constant fear of their lives, and we can enjoy a whiff of that on the M1 after closing-time on a Friday, but wouldn't the sport be more easy to identify with if, as they rounded Beckets or Mount Fuji, a juggernaut was suddenly overtaking in the opposite direction and an old lady sprang out on a zebra.

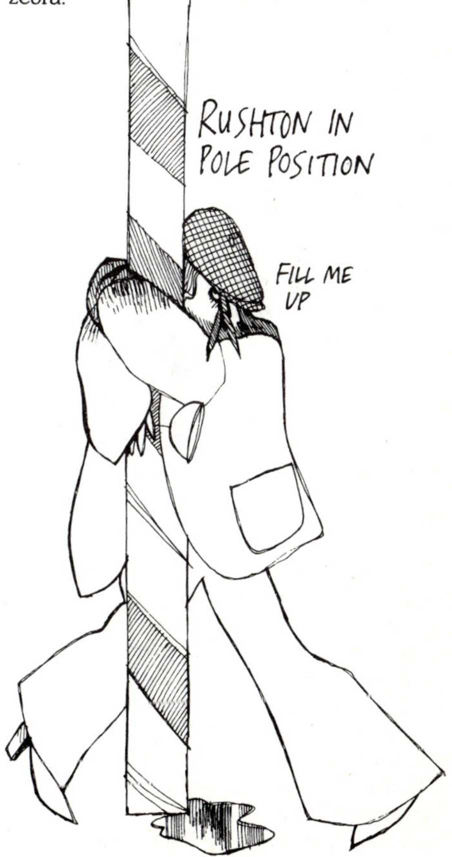

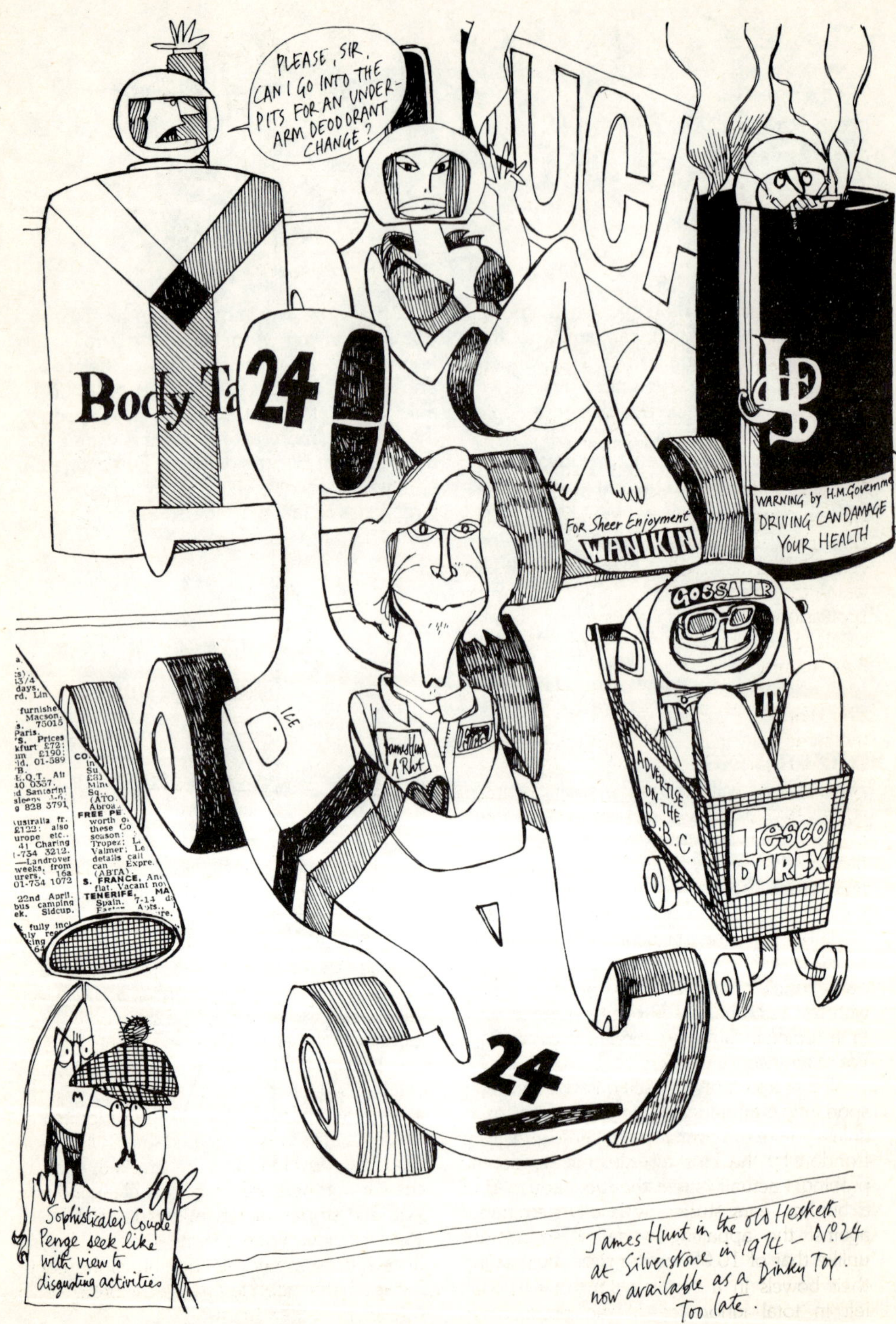

James Hunt in the old Hesketh at Silverstone in 1974 – No. 24 now available as a Dinky Toy. Too late.

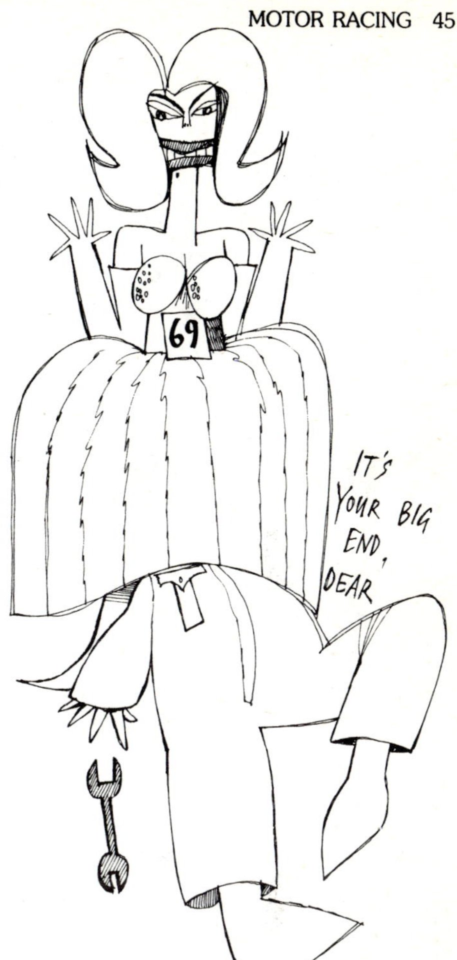

(Cruelty to animals, you will say, idly crippling a hedgehog with your .45. Why don't you hunt juggernauts with a hand-grenade and do mankind a service?)

The average spectator probably doesn't look for the added thrills of Niki Lauda jumping the lights (or Harry Lauda for that matter) or Fittipaldi arguing with a traffic warden. Spectators are a bastardly lot. The Boat Race was never more popular than the year Oxford sank with all hands. Likewise, watch the football crowd rise as, in the most professional of fouls, a practised clogger breaks an opponent's leg in three places. It's their natural delight in witnessing someone else's discomfiture – note the popularity of *The World at War* and *This Is Your Life.* It's the same principle as following fire engines. The only safe sports that enjoy a following are snooker and ballroom dancing in all probability. But even so I remember in a clash between the West Midlands and Home Counties (South) one Doris Rimmer, a plumber's mate from Leamington Spa, being wheeled helpless from the parquet after losing seven yards of tulle. And yet again, in the world of snooker, safe at last you would think, a favourite uncle, Auntie Nell, went after a pink with the rest and did himself no good at all in a pocket. But how that crowd roared! We're an insensitive race.

All that apart, motor racing isn't a spectator sport in that audience participation is minimal, unless you're run over. Having been lured from London by the Hesketh chopper to do my probing, I actually spent the race crouched in a bunker, ears stuffed with oily newspaper against the appalling noise. A sound not unlike that of 10,000 white rhino evacuating their bowels in a very old lorry. I was thus left in total ignorance of the proceedings which, as James Hunt led from start to finish in my host's vehicle, seemed a mite ungracious. I also missed the stirring rendering of that grand old Kop Song by the Massed Choir of the James Hunt Fan Club (sprauncy girls reeking of sump oil and anticipation) which was totally drowned by the roar of traffic. I rather rudely referred to them as 'Pit ponies'.

I like to think I shared in one of motor racing's golden moments, even if I missed the actual race. How bright the future looked as James Hunt was wreathed and filled with champagne. How fine the Hesketh looked, the car not the Lord, white and gleaming with patriotic stripes of red and blue, and not a trace of advertising matter. Alas, as history knows, his summer was short but glorious, but it was a brave effort to take on the brute forces of the sponsored teams.

For that is what the sport is all about. Arranged at the start is a vast commercial for cigarettes, drink, fuel and body talcum so that an unsuspecting stranger might well think motor racing was aimed solely at chain-smoking, totally pissed arsonists and pooftahs.

From the moment the Hesketh chopper landed on the rolling lawns of Hesketh Hall, the Versailles of Northamptonshire, I'd been out of my skull. I'd been teetotal for a year and a half and this was the weekend shares in Johnny Walker soared once more. The Hesketh victory brought on a personal collapse. The prize as far as I could gather from the state of his tent after the race, a thousand people and a cup. He kept the cup. Indeed, he kept the thousand people, but only in drink. After a while they were shipped off, probably to some warehouse owned by *Exchange and Mart* to await Brands Hatch. It's heady stuff – the taste of victory. If you want to know what victory tastes like, it's a mixture of champagne, nicotine and second-hand lipstick. All too much for my over-stimulated system, I hailed a helicopter, headed for the Hall, and had tea and crumpets under the

Rubens. There was a mild suggestion that I should accompany the circus to Monte Carlo, but I felt I'd had enough high living for a decade.

I got a lift back to London in Lord Hesketh's figure-hugging stately mobile home (the only sound you can hear at 80 m.p.h. is the cocktails shaking). I gather Hesketh Racing rides again. You can always flog the Rubens, dear.

Goodbye cruel world, I'm off to join the circuits

If you're going to start racing on the circuits, go (*a*) to a racing stable and have lessons or (*b*) to a driver instructor school. An appraisal course will cost from £10 to £15 and then if it's generally felt you are the stuff that dreams are made of, a course of lessons will be upwards of £100. After about an hour you'll be in a single-seater, and the rest of your life is largely up to you.

Rough Order of Events to the Top

1967

JAMES HUNT: Racing mini which failed R.A.C. scrutineering test. No windows. Tried to persuade R.A.C. that recut, bald tyres were a new secret development.

YOU: Saloon car groups – Minis, Escorts, Renault 5's, etc. – all production cars with safety modifications, namely roller bar, asbestos wall between petrol and engine, full harness seat belts. Sports cars – Again production sports cars with engine tuned to a nicety and the safety aids.

Thence to single-seaters

1968

JAMES HUNT: Formula Ford to Formula Three.

YOU: Formula Ford/1600. A modified Ford Cortina 1600 GT engine. This is the most competitive class, because it's the cheapest.
Formula Ford/2000 As its name suggests.
Formula Three Up to 2 litre production with restrictions as to tuning and engine modifications.

1972

JAMES HUNT: Formula Two Salzburgering and Brazil.

YOU: Formula Two Up to 2 litre racing engine, again to specifications.

1973

JAMES HUNT: Hesketh Surtees F2. Formula One at Monaco. Fourth in British Grand Prix, third in Dutch.

YOU. Formula One The golden biggie. Cars up to 3 litre.

1976

JAMES HUNT: World Champion.

CYCLING

I could perhaps have been a famous cyclist. But I never had the wind. Or the stamina. Or the bicycle for that matter. I bought my last at Harrods one winter afternoon, it was a folding bicycle. To prove its efficiency, it folded twice under me as I weaved down Pont Street. I parked it outside a Russian restaurant in the Kings Road and that was the last I ever saw of it. 'Out again are they, sir?' said the fuzz. 'Who?', I enquired. I could hear him down the 'phone totting up on his knuckle-duster. 'Three years, yes', he said. 'They're out again.' *They* transpired to be a gang of ruthless bicycle thieves that had once roamed Chelsea, and were now back. 'It wasn't locked, I suppose, or chained to the railings?', he asked. Shame-faced I admitted I'd left it loose to idly graze. 'No matter, sir', he reassured me,

'They'd have had it anyway. Railings and all. Into the back of their lorry and off'. Apparently they keep them on ice for a couple of years and then flog them round the universities. It had cost me £35 and I hadn't even had time to insure it. That was it, and Reg Harris felt free to make another of his come-backs.

They're all the rage nowadays, and twice as expensive, but if you cycle at all you could be on the first rung of the ladder to national acclaim – you have the freedom of the road and nothing to fear from the Arabs and their oily businesses. Not strictly true, as I note round Saudi Kensington, the Arabs are more than aware of the snooks cocked at them by cyclists and, by driving extremely badly in large American cars, have cut the numbers down considerably. (*See Camel Riding as a possible riposte in the petrol war.*)

For gentler readers

There is the Cyclists Touring Club, who will give you touring information, third party insurance and legal aid (doubtless for those who nail an unwary Arab chauffeur), a magazine and the names of your local associations, where fellow-pedallists assemble. My only cycling tour, (the very phrase has a flavour of John Buchan serenading a flapper in a punt) was with Richard Ingrams, the editor of *Private Eye.* We decided to cycle from Shrewsbury to London, no great distance you may think. I recall a mosquito-blown night in a tent on the banks of the Windrush, camping in the back garden of a terrace house in Redditch, a game of cricket near Newbury, and finally, after a week of unmitigated agony, taking the train from Oxford to London. Perhaps if we'd had dropped handlebars and considerably less tents and equipment all would have been better.

For harder readers

If you join the British Cycling Federation or a good club, then the Milk Race looms and British success in the Tour de France is long-awaited. I used to fondly imagine the Union Jack proudly emblazoned on my cycling briefs dissolving in the salty sweat, during the leg over the Pyrenees, into a purple badge of courage. It would have clashed, for certain with the yellow jersey. Best at it, of course, are the bloody Belgians – the only nation on earth boring enough to tour France without looking up from the road in front, getting delightfully lost in a Dordogne bistro, or indeed getting a leg over in the Pyrenees.

Under the auspice of the B.C.F. you'll get all the joys of time trials, road races and track races. We have a mild reputation in team pursuit. The British team took a bronze in Montreal. But perhaps the bank managers won the Barber's Shop Quartet Finals in Leeds, my mind occasionally blurs.

A racing velocipede will cost you at least £125, and don't forget the saucy cap, the vest, the thigh-hugging shorts, etc. another £20 or so, unless you take advertising.

MORE ALARMING YET

There is Cyclo-Cross. You can ignore the biblical overtones, I admit it sounds like a station of the Cross, so do Charing Cross and King's, but from a quick thumb through the New Testament I can find no evidence that Our Lord borrowed a bicycle at any moment in His adventures. Nevertheless the principle of cyclo-cross is 'Take up thy bike, and run', so there may be some connection.

It's a fiendish mix of cycling and cross-country running. OPEC can do their worst as far as these lads are concerned. There are 300 clubs in the country costing about £3 per annum to join.

As you have to cart the machine uphill quite often, invariably in thick mud, as the season is sadistically timed from September to February, you'll need an extremely light bicycle with a wide range of gears and no protruberances to catch on hedges, spectators and yourself. Your expert will have his saddle set back slightly both to get more weight over the back tyre for grip and (my balls crawl as I write) for easy mounting and dismounting. A pair of trunks is suggested under your shorts to comfort and support, but even so my eyes are watering. A long-sleeved jersey, gloves and stout shoes that won't come off half-way up a muddy hillock. Daft caps are also *de rigueur* in cyclo-crossing circles.

But, take heart, we compete annually in the World Championships, so fame could be yours. The basics would seem to be a fast start, the offering of 'spirited resistance' to all attempts to pass you, and a final hint – as your blood-stained, mud-encrusted body breaks the tape – if your number has been obliterated, shout it out with your last breath. You are mad.

There is also a form of polo on bicycles. I think we'd all have enjoyed watching a goal from Lord Mountbatten in that unlikely sport.

MOTOR CYCLING

Still laughably dangerous. You could say that at least there's no pedalling but you still wouldn't get me on the back of a motor cycle if you offered me the lead in *Sons of the Wild Ones.* There's the mystique of motor cycling. Rockers, black leather, chains and studs, motorised Younger Brothers, roam the motorways hunting Cortinas instead of buffalo. They roam on great, snorting steeds that, in the same way as Trigger now stands stuffed by Roy Rogers' guitar-shaped pool, are still loved and nurtured in the same unnatural manner.

The sinister nature of the motor cycle is exemplified for me by the Boys in Blue. Plant your honest plod on a motor cycle and he's instantly dragged screaming with pleasure into 1984. Alfred Hitchcock realised that menace, you may remember, early on in *Psycho*, the highway patrolman in brutal shades filling Janet Leigh's car window with dramatic tension. You'd hesitate to ask the time from one of *ours*. Safer to ask the psycho. There may be a heart of gold beneath the helmet and goggles and feet of clay in the jackboots, but it doesn't show. And all the time, his bicycle shouting instructions at itself like a Dalek. Not that our police haven't undergone a distressing change of image since they stood firmly by P.C. Dixon as typical of their behaviour, scoffed at *Z-Cars* for showing policemen drinking beer and getting divorced and other unlikely police behaviour. Today, inspired by *Kojak* and *Starsky and Hutch*, they have turned on 103-year-old George Dixon and identify heavily with *The Sweeney*. The price of liberty is eternal violence.

On the Civil List, Evel Knievel is the patron saint of the motor cycle. St Christopher fell off the back of a Harley Davidson years ago. Were he to attempt the same tricks on horseback, jumping over busloads of sharks or the English Channel he would have been despatched to the glue factory years ago, but as long as it's only he or his machine that is twisted and bent, all's well. Indeed the Erich von Stroheim Memorial Neck Brace has now become as much a status symbol of the motor cyclist as the other Germanic accoutrements.

Even Sir Ralph Richardson, a man I admire enormously despite a lifetime in the saddle has, it must be allowed, frequently been described as 'quirky'.

It's all very well for you to say that this is grossly unfair to the motor cyclops but I feel a lot better.

I'm sure they're sweet and loveable people and firm believers in the sanctity of human life, I simply think they shouldn't be allowed on the roads. The which is why I commend trials-riding, or Moto-Cross to you.

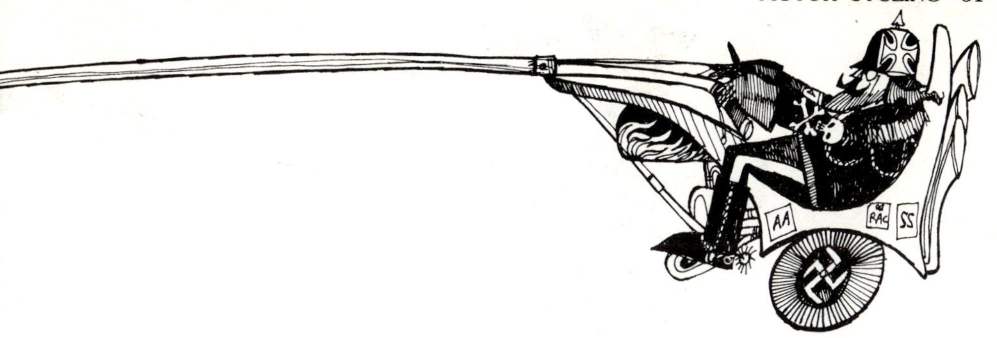

TRIALS

This is the cheapest entrée into the business. For a start it's the only branch in which you can use the same machine that drives me potty on the M4. A secondhand trials bike costs £200-£300. Compare that with £500 plus for a moto-cross bike or £1000 at very least for road racing, added to which you need a car or van and trailer to get the beastly thing to the venue.

As in all categories, you must have an Auto Cycle Union Competition Licence (which costs £2 per annum for a restricted one) and you must join a club. Trials riding concerns skill only, speed is not of the essence, the judges mark you on your ability to cope with different situations and terrain. You'll find yourself pounding over muddy slag-heaps, rocky tracks, dried-up river beds and the like, and I like. It keeps you off the streets. So does –

MOTO-CROSS

Do not panic. You probably imagined yourself running up Ben Nevis carrying your Honda across your shoulders. Not so, but it is no picnic. Nor, in my view, is picnicking, but that's irrelevent. It has been likened to operating a travelling road-drill. Turbulence is another word for it, as in flying Alitalia, or flying genitalia, to be more precise.

I've seen its praises sung as being the only aspect of motor cycling that allows 'wild sliding, high jumping and flat-out speeding'. Very well, but, as that suggests, both you and the machine are going to take a rare pummelling. Indeed, the better and more ambitious you become in the sport, the more expensive it gets in new hardware and breakages. It helps to be mechanical as well as maniacal.

For moto-cross the clothing alone comes to about £100. There are minimum standards and your kit has to be approved by the Auto Cycle Union. An approved helmet sells for £12, goggles for about £5 and face-mask, not unlike an ice hockey goalkeeper's or an extra from *Dr. Who*, cost £2 or so. That's just your head. Apart from which there are now musical helmets, with mini two-way intercom. Speak to your passenger while enjoying your favourite radio programme, and try to remember you are doing a ton up the A1. There's also a rich assortment of bodywork. Shoulder guards, chest guards, leather jeans, gloves and great boots.

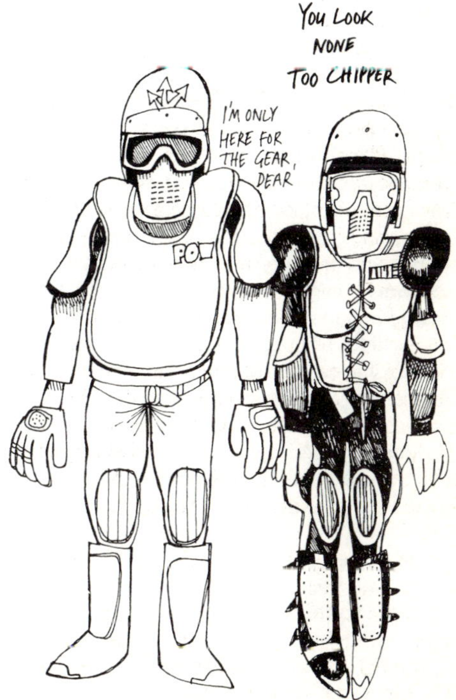

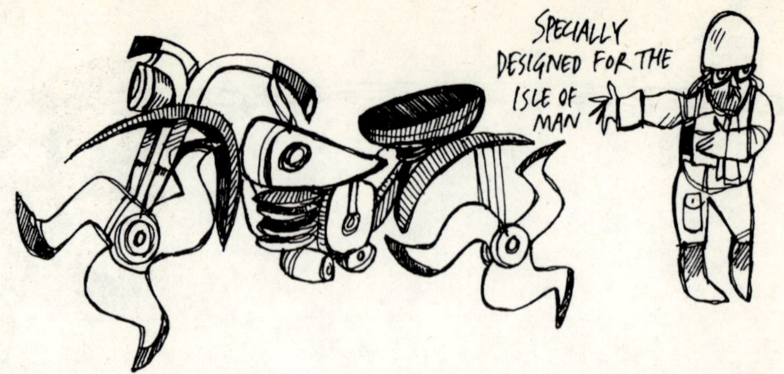

They don't advise over-35s to take up moto-crossing, the bones are brittling. Grass-track racing sounds more the mark. Road Racing, as in the Isle of Man TT, is some distance from the mark, although I suppose it gives the rider a boot to have an open road. It seems a pity to waste it.
Auto Cycle Union, 31 Belgrave Square, London, S.W.1. Mrs L. Hill, The Secretary of the British Schoolboy Motorcycle Association, 18 Glenn Park Crescent, Kings Court, Stroud, Gloucs. (Kids can start aged 6. It's cheaper to keep a pony in the bathroom.)

SPEEDWAY
Almost all the comics as I remember, the wordy ones anyway, the *Hotspur*, *Champion*, *Wizard* and others had at some time or other one hero who was a Speedway rider. I can't think why except that all our comic heroes then were sporting ones, and it's a sport for heroes. Not the comic superheroes of today, who are more concerned with politics, philosophy and hyper-bionics, metamorphosing from good, ordinary all-Americans into gaudily leotarded crypto-Muppets, Thisman, Thatman, Ombudsman and Hitman for the Festival of Light from the Mobster Funbook. I did admire 'Captain America', however, who hung up his stars and stripes, changed his name and burned his costume after Watergate – I think he was on to Nixon before *The Washington Post.* (*Stop Press* – he is now back in his old gear – the Americans are an optimistic people at heart.)

My heroes were 'Rockfist' Rogan, a boxing fighter pilot, once locked in combat with a villainous Farmer Rushton – picture my infant glee. Also a test cricketer suffering from some unknown paralysis picked up in the Matto Grosso which caught up with him at awkward moments like going for the run that would clinch the Ashes. And, of course, Wilson the Wonder-Athlete. I remember him running up Everest in a vest and decent, long, baggy shorts. And the Speedway bloke, another name lost as the grey cells curl up and die. You don't seem to hear so much of Speedway now. Occasionally they show it on television but only, you feel, because Wincanton has frozen solid. A pity really, because I gather we're rather good at it. I blame the Japanese; it makes a change from the Arabs.

. . . THERE'S ALSO AN UP, UP AND AWAY

FLYING

Why not fly, you daredevil? Do pig-stickers have wings? You may well enquire. The best man at the Rushton wedding in Crow's Nest, New South Wales, one Geoff Harvey, once an organist at Westminster Cathedral and now famed Australian band-leader and musician (he slowed to a grinding halt after the first eight bars of *Here Comes The Bride*, and was forced to improvise jazzily), swears by it. For years he has contemplated a flying pianist service for anyone eager for a knees-up round Alice Springs (A Town Like Bruce). It is, he vows, an escape from the pressures below.

Go to a flying school, membership costs about £15 per annum, including insurance, and provided you pass the medical, you'll be aloft in a nonce, under instruction, which comes at £15 and upwards for an hour.

You can start doing the mathematics now. Before you can do the General Flying Test and become the proud possessor of a Private Pilot's Licence (P.P.C., and a fine thing to let drop idly from the wallet if seeking to impress), you must have flown a minimum of 40 hours, 25 of these under instruction and 15 hours alone and unaided. Yes, it will cost at least £650. You must also fly five hours in every 13 months to keep it up, without another test flight. However, you have the Licence for life, the length of which is to come extent your business, and costs £35.

Buying a Plane

A plane will cost you at least £15,000. Look at it this way – that's half the price of a crudely converted ex-stable in Chelsea. Second-hand you could get one for £10,000, am I not trying to be helpful? You could form a small gang (you, Biggles, Ginger, Algie, Amy Johnson, etc.) and split the cost. Further, to help with the expenses – fuel, for instance, costs about 90p a gallon and in the smallest of planes you'll consume about eight gallons an hour – you can hire the snorting bird back to your airfield or flying school for their use. Hangaring costs about £20 for each month.

The Anti-Hangaring Lobby

Join an airfield, for £3 or £4 a month, and hire a plane whenever the urge takes you or you can afford £15 an hour, fuel included. (For as little as 11p which covers insurance, you can take a passenger, and charge them excessively for the thrill.)

I admit it's expensive, but they say it's easier than driving a car, and a deal less crowded. There's no money in it, the rallies and competitions organised by the clubs are only for pots and trophies. However, you could wind up flying Concorde. There's not much future in that, of course.

YOU COULD GLIDE

This could well be more your mark. The British Gliding Assocation, Kimberley House, Vaughan Way, Leicester, will give a full list of the clubs to join, full-time ones, weekends, evenings only, etc. A good, small local one will take you to their bosom for as little as £12 a year. A larger one may want a £20 entrance fee and about £50 a year, but this will include tuition.

Flying charges vary. Some clubs charge for the launch and then for your time in the air, around 5p a minute. Others merely ask for the price of a launch. Eighty pence for a launch on a winch, which sounds rather wonderful and if you're given an aerotow, namely, dragged aloft by an aeroplane and then left to your own devices, that will be about 30p a minute.

The B.G.A. recommend warm clothing, an ability to go for long periods without eating, and a cast-iron bladder. Funnily enough I remember being told by a keen gliding-person that the only way to find out whether you were the right way up in heavy cloud was to spit or piss and if it shot upwards past your goggles, you were upside down.

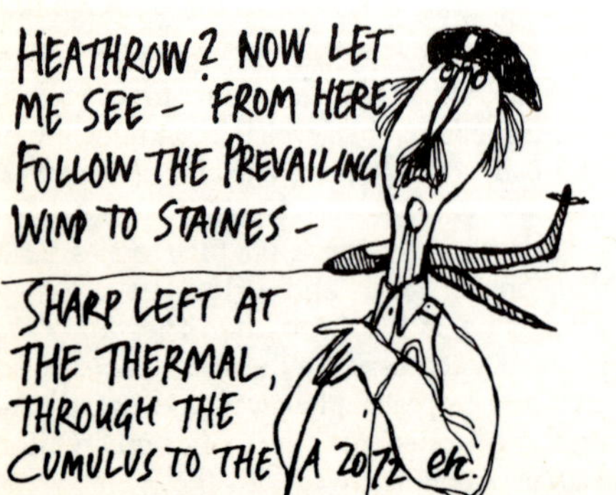

Buying your own glider seems to be an unnecessary way of injecting vast expense into a basically cheap pastime. Second-hand they're at least £3500 and a souped-up new one can come at £12,000. You'll need a trailer too and all that.

However, once you're up there in the wide, blue yonder, you are alone, in total peace, far from the madding telephone, the roar of the traffic and the crowd, the smell of the grease-paint, at one with Mother Nature, and quite possibly upside down.

BALLOONING

It must be great when cornered by golfers or yachting buffs or boozy rugger types to silence the company with a quiet but firm 'I am a balloonist'. This person, they think at once, is clearly intrepid and yet something of a poet.

It's simply you in your basket, your hot air, and your balloon, travelling where'er the wind wills it. The hot air will take you up and down like a lift as your whim wishes, but steering, while possible if you can at some height find a suitable wind going in your direction, is on the whole in God's lap and so are you. One of the happier adjuncts of the pastime is that you have to be followed by a retriever in a car, not the dog, you fool – with suitable trailer, as balloons never land you where you started. This, as you can imagine, has become a sport all its own – balloon-pursuing, and I would imagine as the balloon heads for the wild blue yonder, also road-losing, desperate hooting and cross-country balloon-hunting.

The favoured course would appear to be to buy a balloon. They cost about £2000, but if you gang up with a few others, the cost is cut and you have a built-in team of flight technicians and retrievers. Not too many, or you'll never get airborne.

It's also less expensive to be trained by qualified gentry in your own balloon. To get your licence in Britain, to become a qualified balloon pilot (how fine that would look on a passport), you must have at least 12 hours of dual instruction and a dual test flight, and then a solo flight and there are a few examinations in navigation, airmanship, etc. Medically all they ask is a declaration from you that you can't think of any good reason why it might be dangerous for you to pilot a balloon.

Cameron Balloons of Bristol are the second largest builder of hot air balloons in the world. They made the amazing floating trousers that advertise Levi's Jeans (waist 1160 inches, inside leg 1198 inches, a fact recorded on the label on the waistband) and they have occasional symposia. Fifteen to 20 people, eager to balloon, assemble for a weekend at a pleasant country hotel and for £33 including accommodation, get a thorough grounding, or airing if you like, in ballooning.

Balloons are not difficult to run, they have to be inspected for their Certificate of Airworthiness annually, but Cameron Balloons advertise a rapid spare parts service throughout the world. Where are you going to?

There is ever the possibility of covering some of your expenses by taking advertising, or turning up at the odd fête as something of an effect.

Balloon pilot? I think *my* search has ended.

You and the Elements
PLAYER'S
NAVY CUT
WRONG
40
655

WET BOBS

'Wet bobs' is the ludicrous phrase coined by Etonians and only used by them to describe those who go down to the river for their sporting recreation. It appears quite frequently in *The Times* crossword puzzle, as do their more earth-bound counterparts, the dry bobs. So, of course, does 'Pop', the Eton Mafiosa.

These are the watery sports involving machinery, tackle, planks and impedimenta, which is why you will find swimming elsewhere, which only requires a costume and for the keener brethren an ice-pick. Not that you have to swim in the Serpentine all the year round, it's simply that there are those who do. One of my grandfathers had a cold bath every morning and lived until he was 90. The other enjoyed a bottle of gin and another of Scotch daily and lived until he was 87. A bottle of gin and a hot bath is something else entirely. My word, Mother Nature leads us a merry dance.

SAILING

To refer to it as 'yachting' is apparently uncouth and disgraceful like calling a boat a ship or vice versa. The Olympics refer to it as 'yachting' and moves are constantly afoot to make them change their ways. Hell hath no fury like a sailor irked. Look at Edward Heath. I can come up with only two other similar combinations of the sea and music. One, at the end of *The Marx Brothers at the Circus* when Harpo cuts loose the floating orchestra from their moorings and they were last seen floating past the old 'Queen Mary' in mid-Atlantic. The second the touching rendition of *Abide With Me* played by the Palm Court Orchestra of the *S.S. Titanic* as it sank. Either way, ever as the grand old Clyde Shipyards vanished into an equally watery grave, E. Heath did a great deal to popularise the smaller boat. Funnily enough, I met him at the

1976 Boat Show, with a small Elastoplast stuck to the bridge of his nose, a clear demonstration of the dangers ot shaving on dry land. There can't be much wrong with a man who removes his lavatory door for added speed.

It would be all too easy to write off sailing folk as a gang of hearties clad in smocks and yellow wellingtons, who sound, even in the smallest of talk, as if they're conversing against a Force Nine gale. Terribly true, but too easy. Nor is the Royal Yacht Squadron typical of the breed; with their blazers and flannels, saucy 'Hello Sailor' caps and the rolling gait of an old salt stiff with pink gin.

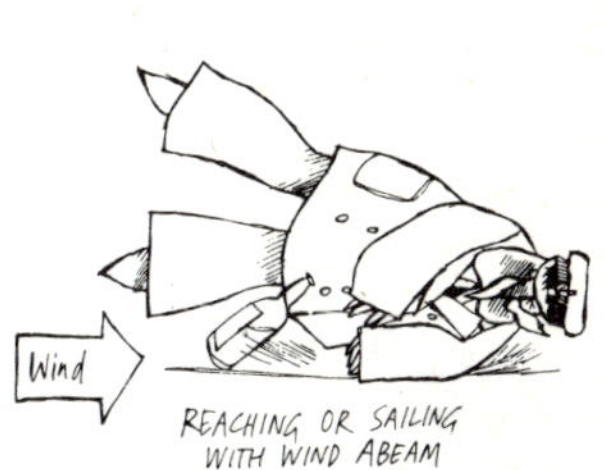

If Bembridge is the place to be, and the yachting fraternity a bunch of laughs and a joy to embrace, how come the increasing popularity of single-handed boating? It seems to be carrying the search for peace and quiet too far. Of course, some years ago there was a knighthood and a bestseller in it, as in Harold Wilson at Number Ten, only less crowded and fraught with danger. Nowadays there's Clare Francis, who has struck a blow for dames at sea, although the damehood hasn't come through yet at time of writing, and has also added a touch of glamour to the proceedings. Sir Francis Chichester and Sir Alec Rose were bold as brass but not pretty men.

It was their activities that inspired me to dwell briefly on what solo activity I could indulge in that would bring instant fame and fortune. As every other form of transport had circumnavigated the globe at some time or other, it occurred to me that a good brisk walk, though lengthy, might capture the public imagination. Always though, over my head hung the sorry picture of myself, laden with maps, haversacks, tents, visas and a change of socks, only some hundred odd yards from the start, but gasping already. I was passed by cheerful, smiling dignitaries, mayors and aldermen, Grub Street hacks and photographers, etchers from *The Illustrated London News*, and kids with flags and bunting as they ambled quietly homewards from the celebratory blast-off.

One small tip I have garnered is to forget the Sydney-Hobart Race, and volunteer to crew a craft home from Hobart to Sydney, by which time no one gives a stuff and the fine ales and wines of Australia flow like God's nautical beard. Indeed, the one value of being known in sailing is the chance available of picking

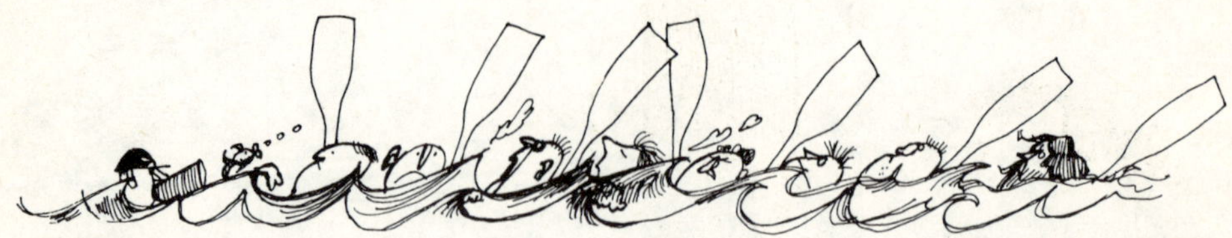

up and delivering boats. Particularly if they're sponsored. There's an increasing amount of that about.

One larger tip. If asked to embroil yourself in a round-the-world trip, pick one of the fast boats – this means a week's recouping in Rio and Honolulu as opposed to an afternoon if with the slower brethren.

If asked to lash yourself to Norman St John Stevas in a round-the-world three-legged race – forget it.

If you feel the call of the water, and the murky, oil-slicked, effluent-packed liquid is said to flow through our veins, which explains perhaps our sudden tiredness, find a good sailing school (particularly one that offers a week or so's package, giving the full flavour). Write to *the Royal Yachting Association, Victoria Way, Woking, Surrey GU21 1EQ*. Would that be the Woking famed in so many a shanty, whence Drake sailed forth to trounce the Armada after bowling on Woking Hoe? Try them anyway. And also ask them why they're not called the Royal Sailing Association. Ho, Ho, Ho. It's not a cheap pastime, though, of course, you can gauge the size of your craft to the size of your bank balance.

ROWING

Think of the pleasures of a quiet row on a boating pond or river, particularly a river. I'm very fond of rivers. Ah, the sweet innocence of the waterside folk.

'By the river, Rat and Badger
Explain the mysteries of Flage-
Lation to the startled Mole
Who much prefers Toad in the hole.'

The nearest you can get to a gentle row or punt in sport is individual sculling, as long as you studiously avoid competition. Even so, by the very nature of the craft, you'll discover muscles you never realised were present while idling in second on the Serpentine.

My old Alma Mater was a famed rowing school, which was fine by those who didn't row as it kept the mountainous lunks off the cricket field. They would set off for the river in grubby vests and enormous white baggy reinforced shorts, leaving the sweet, new-mown grass untrammelled by their leaden feet. What went on down by the riverside I never explored too closely, they would return grubbier yet, vomit-stained and lifeless, gasping out references to 'feathering light', 'giving her ten', and then explosing the myth of this inter-sexual athleticism by confessing to 'upping ratings'. Hello, sailor again!

We used to have bumping races annually and those I did patronise. I've mentioned the joys for the spectator of watching Oxford sink all those years ago. I can see no other reason why people still spend time watching the Boat Race. The result is invariably inevitable, and aesthetically it's not up to much, but I see Ladbroke's are taking up sponsorship of the Race. Perhaps they'll insist on a first-rate collision by Watney's Brewery or something to liven up the public's jaded palate.

Bumping races, as the name suggests, do

contain elements of crowd-pulling violence. Some 20 boats staggered down the Severn at equal distances would, on the blast of a shot-gun, set off after the boat in front in full cry, their aim to rap their prow against the bow or better through the back of the cox of the preceeding craft. They would then move above that boat the next afternoon and embark in pursuit of fresh prey. They could of course be savaged by their vengeful conquest of the day before. It was always jam-packed with action. At the end of four days you had a charming chart, a sort of graph to demonstrate the ups and downs of the top twenty. Most attractive on this card would be a double-bump where one fortunate boat by-passed the

wreckage of two others who had bumped, and succeeded in brutalising the lads previously three boats ahead. All that and the excitement of the chase, as supporters ran along the banks blowing trumpets and ringing bells. The coaches, oblivious to all but the antics of their crew, cycled furiously over entwined lovers or sunning pensioners, roaring like bullocks through megaphones.

An added incentive to spectating is the occasional opportunity of seeing someone catch a crab. Digging his blade too deep into the water, spectacular effects can be created, I have seen oarsmen ejected feet into the air and thrown into the river as though the cox had pressed a button and fired their sliding-seat. Sliding-seats, incidentally, can cause appalling accidents. Essential parts can be entrapped in their jaws.

If you live near a river then there will in all likelihood be a club for you to join along its banks somewhere. I've always had a soft spot for boat houses, essentially practical buildings garaging as they do on the ground floor the skiffs, the fours and the eights, and with ample scope above for an attractive bar and verandah from which either to watch the poor souls at it over a large gin, or the sun setting over the gentle, gleaming water and the cruising swans over another large gin. Water is so much more interesting to look at for long periods than grass. In fact, grass can be quite dull.

A club subscription will cost anything between £10 and £20 per annum. No previous experience is necessary, fitness will clearly be seen to be an advantage, weight, strength and height are helpful, but coaching will be included in the sub. There is no shortage of gentlemen only too eager to cycle recklessly in your wake, bawling orders and abuse. If you are small and vicious, you can of course sign on as a cox. Driving eight men twice the size of you to an early grave, as they are but putty in your hands, could well fill the cup of the shorter bastard. Remember, however, short-arse, the fate of Mrs Mao who was accused of causing the decease of the Chairman with terminal nagging.

The basic kit is shorts and a vest, and a tracksuit or the like, some £20 or so. The rest will be provided. The more exotic kit (as worn by ageing ex-oarsmen now mothballed in the Stewards Enclosure at Henley) in other words the light blue caps, the shocking pink blazers of Leander, faded boaters and jaundiced flannels, is another bag altogether. Downing Pimms to the strangled strains of *The Pirates of Penzance* from the bandstand, they whoop with pleasure as they sight some dimly remembered old adversary to whom the years

have been even less kind. And while thinking perhaps that if only the age they are so desperately trying to recapture still existed, then their shares in Consolidated Punts and Wind-up Gramophones would still be burgeoning proudly in the F.T. Index, they piss incontinently in their yellowing trousers and dampen some corner of an English field that is forever foreign to the rest of us. 'Olly! Olly! The Hall!' they cry, but then so perhaps did dodos.

All that apart I still think, as I thought all those years ago, it's an excellent pastime for the ball-blind, and most pleasurable for the observer.

There are about 580 clubs in the country – their addresses can be obtained from the *Amateur Rowing Association, 6 Lower Mall, London W.6.* Ladies too can row, though the more sentitive may shy at the volley of *double entendre* about oars and rowlocks and the inevitable cox. Be prepared also for vast thighs.

CANOEING

There are two types of canoe you may wish to master, both easily recognisable if you were swept off your feet as a kid by the glamour of the Mounties. I was more into the Foreign Legion myself, preferring warmer climes and reckoning eighth-rate French cuisine to be still superior to most Canadian hard tack, pemmican and the odd elk. If, as I was saying, you leant more towards *Fosdyke of the Yukon* or the like, you will have seen at some time or another a villainous Eskimo apparently legless, armed with double-bladed paddle escaping in his kayak. He will be pursued by the more upright Mountie, eager to maintain the 100 per cent record of man-getting established by that Force. He will be half-kneeling in the more traditional canoe, paddling with a single blade. There are variations but these are the two still in most popular use.

There are some 300 clubs affiliated to the *British Canoe Union (70 Brompton Road, London SW3 1EX)*, all quite inexpensive. Once equipped with either a general purpose canoe (£50-£75, paddle £5-£10) or a more expensive racing canoe (£100-£300, paddle £15-£50) there are a number of directions in which to paddle it.

For sheer pleasure, simply tour our rivers and canals idly drifting from pub to pub, skilfully evading the odd weir, the incompetent hire cruiser and the snorting juggernautical gin palaces. If keen for competition, there is straight sprinting which would seem dullish or – and this may be the one for you, slalom racing.

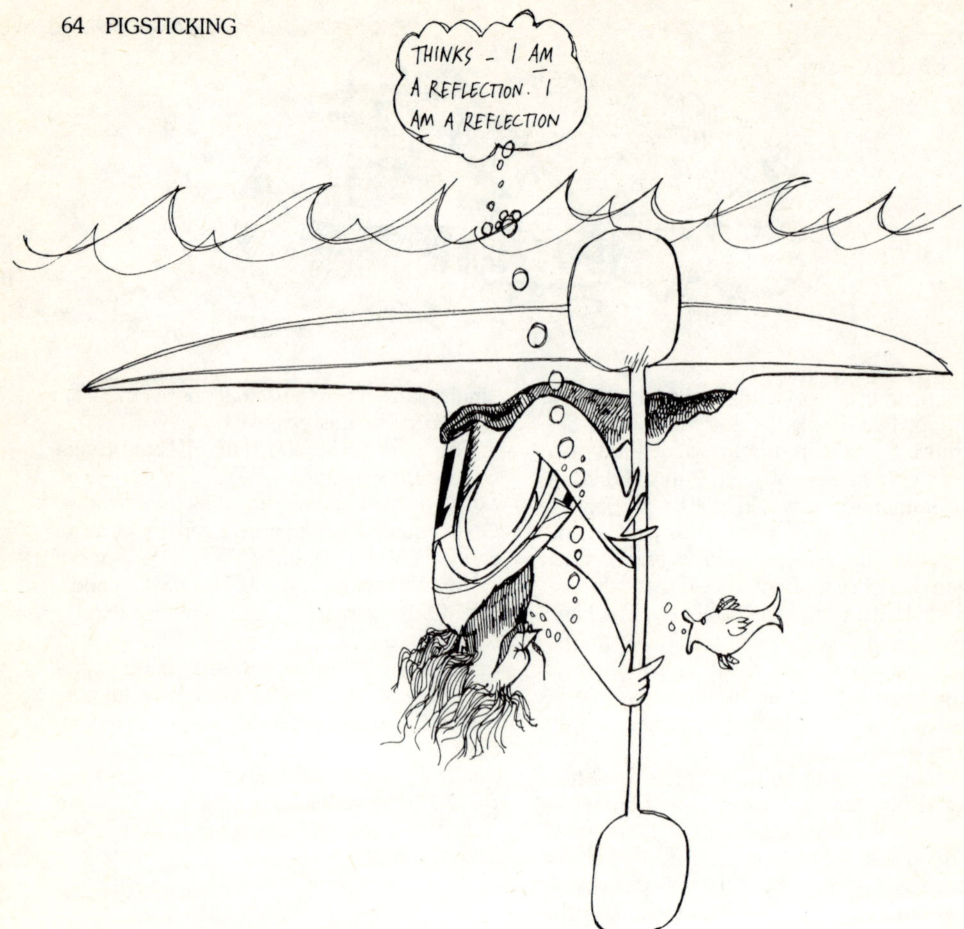

This is normally performed in mini-rapids. Here come the Mounties again, with fast, seething water and assorted rocks, obstacles and death-traps. I well remember the Beeb cutting from Frank Bough to the British Slalom Canoe at the Munich Games. Onto the screen popped a close-shot of an upturned craft and two paddle-less souls in crash-helmets and life-jackets (£8 and vital) swimming dementedly for the bank through the foaming, swirling currents. 'This', said the commentator blandly, 'could well jeopardise Britain's chances of a canoeing gold'.

WATER-SKIING

For some reason Britain is terribly good at this and consistently wins medals in world and European championships. I can't think of any obvious feature in the British character that explains this happy knack – our imperviousness to cold, perhaps? But our sense of balance is appalling, look at the Trade Deficit. There is no record of any early monastic order experimenting with Christ-like aqua-strolling. Anyway, there we are, the question is how about you? Perhaps the best place to start would be on holiday at some resort, preferably abroad with the added incentives of sun, flatter sea and the dogged determination to succeed and not make an utter twit of yourself in the presence of foreigners. It will cost quite a lot for what will seem a brief session, but if you've never done it before, it will seem a lifetime. Many get up the first time and can never understand why there are those who are always dragged face-foremost at pace through the briny cursing roundly. Once you have the trick though, and quite a lot depends on your tutor, it's like bicycling, you never really lose it. It's the thighs that suffer.

Back from holiday and keen to better yourself, find your nearest club by writing to the *British Water Ski Federation, 70 Brompton Road* (again), *London SW3 1EX*. There's plenty of water about, particularly now that they're filling up vacant gravel pits all over the place, and 130 clubs, with subs varying from £5 to £100. Here you'll get the chance to learn the tricks and perhaps a shot at going up and well over ramps, which looks perilous, but must be more interesting than buzzing aimlessly around the bay in ever-decreasing circles until you fall off or run out of petrol.

The kit is pricey, but most of it can be hired or borrowed from the club. The one thing you may wish to invest in, and necessary I would have thought while circling a gravel-pit in winter, is a wet-suit. Someone else's wet-suit doesn't sound very appetising, but your own plus skis and a life-jacket will cost upwards of £100. I should think the life-jacket is absolutely essential, having watched some Americans at speed. When they became detached they were bouncing over water, hard as concrete, at about 80 m.p.h., somersaulting and cartwheeling and winding up prostrate and bobbing, lost to the world while the Red Cross craft closed in.

Our champions, I would add finally, are very young, many in their teens. That's me gone on two scores, approaching senility and sinking.

SUB-AQUA

If you keep sinking, you may say, why not then go in for some underwater activity while you're down there. There is some truth in this. I swim quite strongly underwater, as long as my breath holds out, but this wouldn't be looked upon as sufficient by the British Sub-Aqua Club. They insist on an ability to swim and

Jane Russell in Underwater *(John Sturges, 1955) which had an underwater première in Florida.*

there's a test before you can join a club. Once again this is the cheapest way to learn, there are about 550 in the country, the B.S.A.C. will reveal all from their headquarters in this seemingly waterlogged building at *70 Brompton Road, London SW3 1EX.*

The natural sequence of events would seem to be about 30 hours in the pool and the classroom, a test or two, and then it's heigh-ho for the open water. Clubs organise weekend dives either at sea or in a lake or old gravel-pit. The West Country seems to be Mecca. Many of the clubs own a boat which you will have to pay towards for the day and, of course, cover your expenses for travel and accommodation. The club may be able to come to some arrangement about the latter.

I can't imagine much joy emerging underwater in a gravel-pit, unless you collect old gravel or need it for the drive, but jollity abounds under the sea. Apart from harpooning sea-urchins and fellow members, there is underwater photography, I have a delightful study of Jane Russell in flippers, you may be luckier. There are archaeological studies to pursue, and Atlantis to be found yet. I tend towards the theory that it's in the sub-sub-basement of Venice, shortly of course to be joined by that most beautiful of all cities. You, in your aqua-lung, will soon be one of the few tourists who can enjoy an amble through the Doge's Palace. There are any number of wrecks to explore but they invariably belong to someone else, so exploration is as far as you can go, no nicking cannons to decorate your freshly-gravelled driveway.

Your basic kit, for the first 30 hours snorkelling anyway, will be mask, tube and fins (their word for flippers), which will set you back about £7. If you are absolutely determined to be the first to set his flipper on Atlantean soil, then you'll need the cylinder, the depth gauge, weights, belt, knife and wet-suit which is some £150's worth. Refilling the cylinder costs little.

For pure psychedelia I gather the Great Barrier Reef of Australia is it. You could pause there perhaps on your round-the-world underwater sponsored walk. Your name will be a legend yet.

OCTOPUSH

This certainly came as something of a shock to my system and proves conclusively that fact is considerably stranger than even the most lunatic reaches of fiction. Having conceived the game of kickfish for the underwater Land of Flüt, in which, as you may read, (*see Football*) a great rubber squid is flippered into the opponents' fishing net, fact has caught up with me once again. It happened oddly enough with Durex. 'What game is *this?*' you cry, ever-hopeful of donning the red, white and blue prophylactic and taking the gold for Britain in the Blue Olympics. It is simply that to illustrate the amazing nature of sponsorship I invented for motor racing the Tesco/Durex, which I thought had a ring to it, and was as unlikely as my being linked with Harold and Marcia in what is romantically termed the Eternal Bermuda Triangle. Not so, Durex entered motor racing and the B.B.C. went spare, though why I cannot imagine. They're better for you than cigarettes, unless smoked.

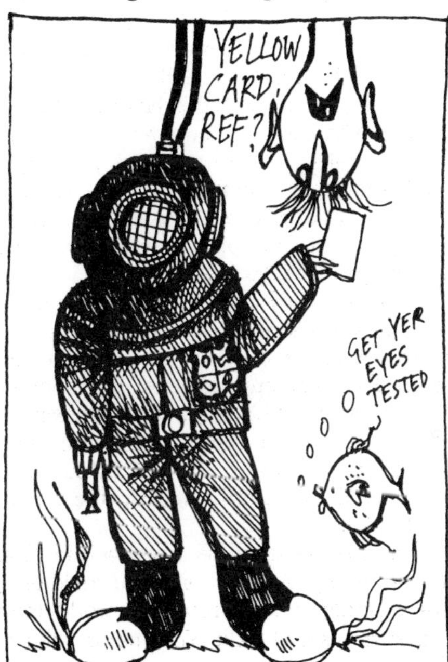

Suffice to say there is a sub-aqua sport called octopush, in which the participants push a squid along the bottom of the octopush pool with a pusher. The object of the game is to propel the said squid into the scoring area, the gulley, and score a gull. It is not recommended by the British Sub-Aqua Club as a spectator sport. It's very hard to render a rousing chorus of *You'll Never Walk Alone* underwater, and the scarves and favours get damp.

They are hoping shortly to start international competitions, so I put it to you that here may well be your chance to represent Old England underwater. It adds a whole new meaning to 'taking a dive in the penalty area'.

SURFING

'It is a remarkable fact that once tried surfing becomes an obsession and the more one becomes involved with it, so it becomes a philosophy – a way of life.'

CARL THOMSON *from Surfing in Great Britain*

It's good to know it happens here at all, let alone the fact that the honest Brit has seen the point of the exercise, we so often miss it. Look what we did to hamburgers. Surfing isn't just standing on a plank and heading for the beach on the seventh wave, it's mind-blowing on the wind, my friend. The Incas used to surf, thence it spread via the Polynesians through the Pacific, and finally the Hawaiians let the rest of us in on it. You have to admit that's a

TAKING GAS - SWALLOWING OCEAN
LUMBERPILE - COLLISION
LUNCHED
OUT TO LUNCH } VAST WIPE-OUT
KOOK - OFFENSIVE REFERENCE TO NOVICE
BOOMER - (A HUGE WAVE) OR BIG STOKER
BUMPS - GNARLED SOLES AND KNEES OF OLD HAND (OR FOOT)
BAGGIES
HANGING FIVE - (TEN IF ALL TOES ASSEMBLE AT FRONT)

livelier start to a sport and pastime than monks or fat Japanese executives. It is a cult, he enunciated carefully.

Although dominated by the Americans and the Australians, the sport is spreading. So are the Australians, of course, their rusting, multi-coloured Dormo-vans are parked everywhere, usually for sale. They have become the new Lost Tribe. But philosophers to a man they are, roaming the globe like the legendary King Pellinore in pursuit of the Questing Beast, ever searching for the ultimate wave, rooting sheilas as they go, cracking their tinnies of cold gold and butting out their scoobies on a thousand beaches. Grabbing their sticks and getting into a nice 50-foot left-hand break, they philosophise the while, 'Shit a brick, if I can get me Makaha lace-ups off, she'll be apples'.

There are more things in heaven and earth, Horatio, than are dreamt of in your philosophy. Too bloody true, mate, but not many.

The British Surfing Association know what clubs there are. These organise weekend trips to the beach, which they call 'surfaris'. They also organise coaching and courses. By joining a club or the Association you get third party insurance, no bad thing as surf-boards on the loose can be deadly for the unsuspecting paddler.

There are surfing holidays, mostly in Cornwall, where they'll teach you the joys of surfdom, practical and philosophical. Prices vary, but Skewjack Village at Sennen near Land's End charge £27 per week per person for everything except food (tuition, loan of board, transport to beach, nightly discos, film shows, etc.) Book early, the Summer of 1977 was booked up by the end of February.

Apparently you can pick up the basics in a week, provided that you're not blessed with total ineptness, but to be really good you must start young, peaks are reached at around 20. It can still be enjoyable on the lower slopes, however, so don't be discouraged. If accused of being a 'ho-dad', a senile surfer, remind them that no way of life is perfect that can lead to a series of the most urky movies Hollywood ever produced concerning the activities of one 'Gidget' played as I recall by Sandra Dee, or very nearly. Buster Keaton was in one or two, poor lost genius.

A custom-built board (or 'stick') will cost around £100, and can be a thing of intense beauty. Off the peg, they come at about £60 or £70. Boards hot from one mould, 'pop-outs' are fine for learning on and cost £35-£40. You may well find a wet-suit necessary in our uncertain climes, they cost £35 and upwards.

British Surfing Association, 18 Bournemouth Road, Parkstone, Poole, Dorset.

DRY BOBS

TOBOGGANING

How long ago it seems since I belted down a snow-clad cliff on a chair-back, narrowly avoiding total immersion in a river I'd forgotten about at sea-level. Trays were quite good, but chair-backs were better. Lads with toboggans were viewed as having more of their parents' money than sense, after all it doesn't snow that much in Our Green and Increasingly Unpleasant.

To get into the big-time you have to be able to take four months off a year to practise on the Continent. If you are gainfully unemployed, rich as Croesus and desparate for something to do, the British Racing Toboggan Association run a week's course in Austria each November to suss out the talent. You pay for clothing and third party insurance, for travel and hotel, they provide the luge (not a mechanical lavatorial aid but in fact the tobogganing vehicle). What they want are young persons eager to make a career of it.

About 35 people attend the course, so if you fulfil the financial qualifications, you could make the team. Apart from money, however, as I mentioned, youth is the other necessity. Apparently it's inadvisable to start after 28 as the G-Force on the ageing head is tremendous and no good at all for said head, less good the longer the tooth. The toothless head doesn't stand an earthly. You must also be extremely fit. Being broke, 40 and gasping, I know where I stand.

Nevertheless think of the children. The B.R.T.A. in order to encourage the youth of Britain, particularly kids, is trying to fix up exchanges with children in good lugeing areas so that our offspring can have a decent crack at it. The children from the lugeing areas, while here, can of course be indoctrinated into the joys of darts and bar billiards, thus while our lot prosper on the slopes, Continental tobogganers become a thing of the past. This way lies gold aplenty.

It is expensive though, even if it's not as expensive as the bobsleigh which can cost over £4000 a year. Ho, ho, ho, and Bob's your long-lost uncle in Australia who's discovered uranium in his sheep-dip, otherwise no chance. Every bob run costs £4-£5 and is over in a flash or meaty crunch, so if you do six runs a day the bill mounts. Toboggan runs cost but a falling pound.

British Racing Toboggan Association, 82 Fir Tree Road, Banstead, Surrey.

BOBSLEIGHING

This you can write off totally I would think. Nobody's particularly interested in you unless you're extremely well off and have all the time in the world. The Association run courses and trips in Europe and will look at you, and presumably your bank account and your diary, but won't want to know if you only intend to turn up once. (£300 or over.)

Strong, athletic people they have in mind. The start is so important that to qualify you should be able to run 100 metres in under 10 seconds, and at the same time be powerful enough to move the bob at pace. With four aboard it weighs 630 kilos. 'A very heavy animal', said a bobber. Olympic standard sprinters and hurdlers they need, with powerful shoulders. Goodbye.

Cheering Note

Join the Army, they organise bobbing outings, but you still have to do it on leave and pay your way. Prince Michael of Kent does it.

SKI-BOB

This is cycling in the snow – the principle behind it being why stand up and ski when you can sit down and ski? There is, God bless it who'd have guessed, a *Ski-Bob Association of Great Britain* (sub £3) at *Marwood House, Colville Road, Acton, London W3*. If you can ride a bike, you can ride a bob-ski, they say proudly, the only snag being our lack of snow again. You can do it, however, on the artificial ski slopes and down the Matterhorn if the gypsy in your soul is out of his skull and sick to death of selling clothes-pegs outside Harrods.

It's a young sport, which is encouraging, and there are world championships yet, in which we come nowhere, which is discouraging but when you come to think of it hardly surprising. It's surprising how few emergent African nations loom large in the winter Olympics. Perhaps we should stick to sports we know that suit our weather like mud-wrestling. Or forget about world championships and when blessed with snow, cycle on it for the joy thereof.

SKIING

There are a few snags about skiing for the average Briton unless you happen to live at the foot of the Cairngorms. Otherwise it's possibly 14 days per year in Switzerland, France or Italy on a package, and not again until the same time next year if you can make

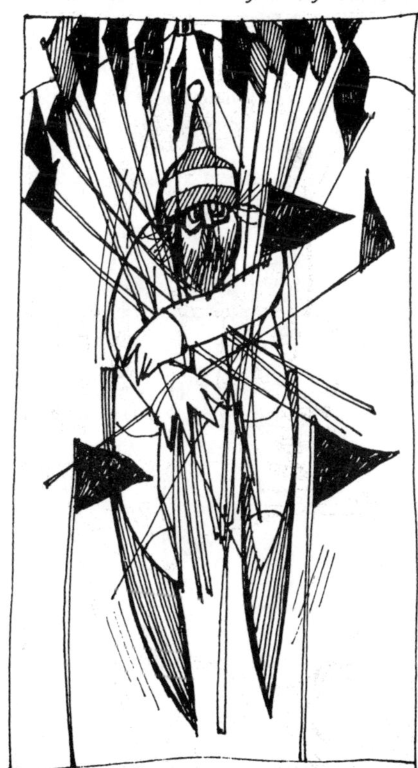

it, and if not it's a long time between outings which may explain our lack of success over the years on skis.

It may be possible for you to get to Scotland more often, it can work out as expensively as going abroad, Goddammit it *is* going abroad. (There's something the matter wi' Glasgee, it's devolving round and round.) Added to which, the conditions are less certain. There is, on occasion, good snow and sun, but more often than not it's very cold, little or no snow, a limited variety of runs, crowded and not a bar to be seen on the mountain. Abroad, at least, if weather turns ugly there are mountain retreats where sorrows can be drowned in *gluwein* or steins of foaming lager.

I was driving through Scotland one January with son Toby, and I thought we might pause at the Cairngorms and whip up a light interest in winter sports. That day, however, it would have been like shooting the rapids. We tried to get there. God knows we tried to get there. Actually even He may not as visibility was nil, rain was teeming down and even with the added advantage of Omniscience it can't have been that easy to pick out one and a half loonies driving at about 2000 feet against a mini-typhoon.

'It's a lizard', Toby said at one stage, meaning blizzard, and giving me further cause for alarm. I will confess the daftest sight I ever saw was a man in full skiing regalia standing, skis in hand, under a failed umbrella.

Skiing Abroad

It will cost you more, but your chances of getting snow to ski on are much better. The weather will be better. Shop around for a good package. The best will include lessons, ski pass for the lifts, hire of skis and the like, all at cut rates. Look at the last-minute holidays advertised on the back page of *The Times* – here lie bargains.

Pick the right country. Switzerland, France and Austria are deeply jet-set and very expensive. Andorra, Spain and Italy are cheaper and less chic. You may only be there for the après-ski. Personally, I would only go to a ski resort with my leg already in plaster. The drink will be delightfully cheap in one of the duty-free resorts in Andorra or Italy. Fresh air, exercise and alcohol, what more do you need? More alcohol, nurse.

If you're starting, it's mildly foolish to dress up like the Aga Khan or Monsieur Killy. Hire a decent pair of waterproof trousers, as you'll be sitting in the snow a good deal. You may have an anorak, again, they can be hired. Thick socks, ski-gloves, woollies, goggles and sunglasses, and a sensible warm hat. Hire the ski-boots, but take a sensible pair of rubber-soled shoes, hideous accidents occur *off* the slopes – people falling over in the road.

Dry Ski Slopes

Not teetotal, do not alarm yourself. I refer to those artificial slopes, those large trellis-works of criss-crossed nylon bristle or whatever, that are springing up all over the country, and down which, apparently, thumbs are easily trapped and broken. However, they are a good way to learn and a sensible place to go prior to your ski holiday for a quick refresher course and work-out for those long-lost muscles. *The Ski Club of Great Britain, 118 Eaton Square, London, SW1 9AF* will reveal all about them. Lessons are individual or grouped and cost about £10 for half-a-dozen. You can ski there for an hour, equipment often included, for £1.50. Why do people go to Switzerland? Winter at the Crystal Palace.

YOU'RE out on your OWN

ME MACDONALD

ME JANE

HOT AND COLD RUNNING WATER SPORTS

SWIMMING

If you can swim, and this is of course the first essential, and if you wish now to take it up full-time and slip into the flippers of David Wilkie, then the Planet Ocean is at your feet. In fact, you're probably far too old for competition swimming. Here is a simple test. If you have managed to read and understand this paragraph to date, then you are over the hill, past it and there is only one direction left for you to swim in. That is towards France, it is not too late to become a Channel swimmer, though I think you'll have to make it to and fro across the Channel twice in each direction to enjoy any sort of acclaim. If you're fat, however, impervious to cold, possess a bathing costume, goggles, a friend with a rowing boat, and several buckets of lard, join the *Channel Swimming Association, Moorings, Alkham Valley Road, Folkestone, Kent* (£3 per annum). This is, we are told, the only genuine club, beware of imitations. No one has swum the Irish Sea, yet, nor indeed the Atlantic. There are still openings left for fame and fortune.

Fame and fortune come less easily in the swimming pool. Inspired doubtless by the Olympic fame and resultant fortunes of Johnny Weissmuller, by far the greatest and only truly inarticulate Tarzan, many a swimmer since has pictured himself gracing that rôle. It was mooted that Mark Spitz, fresh from seven golds in the Munich Baths, would slip easily into the part. Memories are short in swimming, though. I blame the chlorine which I know causes my head to ache. I saw the report of an interview with Mark Spitz after he'd been taken over by a consortium of money-makers. They actually answered all the questions. An earnest, crew-cutted P.R. man explained that these were early days in the creation of the Spitz image and that he was not yet 'programmed to talk'. Now, as far as I can tell, he is simply a name sewn into the odd pair of second-hand trunks.

One of the sadder sights of Montreal, I found, was at the Olympic Pool. They would announce the next event and a motley line of persons in bathcaps and dressing-gowns, clutching little bags to them would march to a tune not unlike *The Teddy Bears' Picnic* to the starting line. They looked like nothing so much as the queue for the bathroom early any morning in a crowded Y.M.C.A. Sadder yet, were the East German girls stripping, revealing flat, hard chests and shoulders like legs of

The author being greeted by television and press after almost completing a width of the Olympic pool, Droitwich. Only the weight of a damp hat prevented total success. Here he has just come up for the third time and the entire Eamonn Andrews and his red book can be seen flashing before him.

lamb. 'Look at those deltoids!' the commentators would cry, and I would have to make an excuse and leave.

This seems to be the shape of gold medallists to come. As you're senile in swimming terms at 20, I can't believe it's a shape worth getting into; but then I can't swim anyway. (I blame the chlorine again, my natural inclination towards sinking, my pathological dread of dead horses. It's silly not to be able to swim, after all Australians can crawl before they can walk.) The A.S.A. (Amateur Swimming Association) say that, 'swimming is essential and as easy as walking, once you coordinate the body movement'. One of the bodies with the less coordinated movements is the A.S.A., so that if you seek gold for Britain, go to the U.S.A. Wilkie was our first since 1908. Pre-Tarzan yet!

Swimming couldn't be easier or cheaper. There are pools all over the place, and the sea if all else fails. One looming adjunct I might end by suggesting is synchronised swimming, aquatic dance routines, underwater sambas and Busby Berkeley is Alive and Well and Living at Cardiff Baths. There are clubs for this, and I might learn to swim, if only to be able to lean nonchalantly against the bar gossiping about Esther Williams.

SKATING

Young and foolish we were then in those dear, dead days at Queen's Ice Rink, Bayswater. The main pleasure I remember of my skating days was propelling myself along the rink-side by seizing young girls' breasts and launching myself at speed towards the next pair. This is pre-permissive society, but they were jolly girls, sitting ducks on skates, but uncomplaining, and many the bond struck up as you hurtled into them, all hands, shouting, 'Sorry about this'. The hard part I remember was cementing the relationship as this invariably involved walking to the bar and back with a couple of pints and with skates still on. This grew progressively difficult as the night

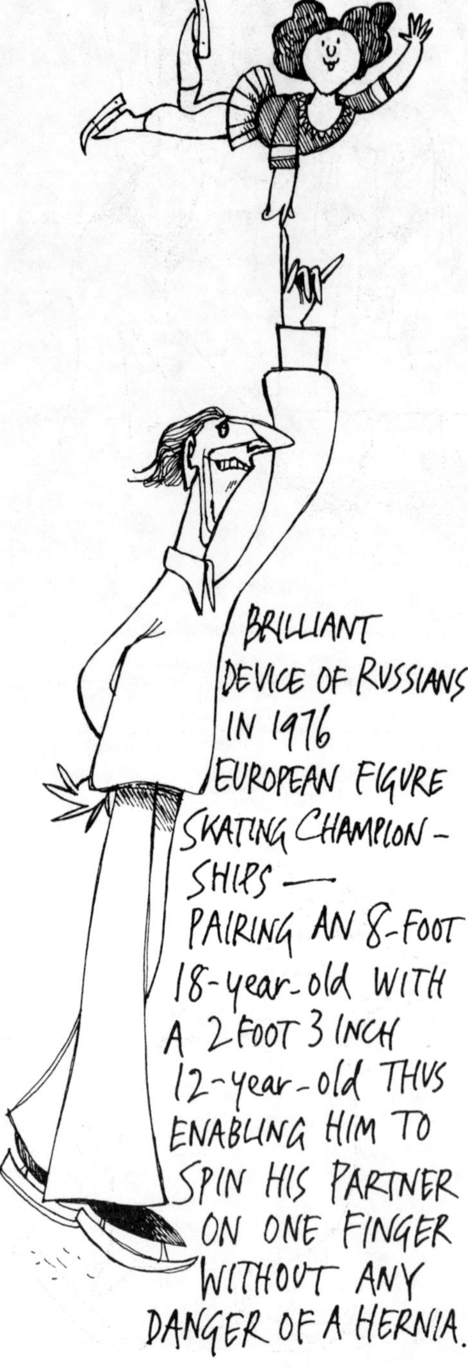

lengthened, and the pain in the ankles was excruciating.

There were dangerous moments. As you grew more skilful you moved away from the bosoms that clung to the side, onto a circuit that surrounded the centre of the rink where the élite pirouetted and sprang. I was nearly cut to pieces one night when pushing off from a massive platform, a huge girl from Kilburn, I fell heavily in the path of a fast-approaching chorus-line of skaters, linked as if to sing *Auld Lang Syne* and with clearly no chance of disentangling themselves prior to mincing Rushton. I hurled myself towards the centre crashing into a right brace of smart-arses, *he* foolishly whirling as he held *her* aloft. I think I downed about seven in my skid, blades whistling about my head like enraged Gurkhas. Perhaps one of them, though, was the young John Curry, and that moment persuaded him that there was insufficient room in this country to skate in, unless you train at five o'clock in the morning, and that it would be best to go to America to cultivate the art in peace. If it was, then he owes me something of a debt, as does Britain, but I don't think he was born then. (Stout party relapses into deep gloom.) Albeit-moresoever, he has now gone into the Theatre.

Most rinks have teachers and clubs attached (lessons from pros range from 90p-£1.50 for the quarter-hour). Entrance for a session is about 40p and you can hire a pair of skates for a couple of old florins. Mine never fitted properly which made the trip to the bar perilous in the extreme. So buy your own if you're going into it seriously. Posh ones cost you about £45. You'll need two pairs, of course, if you figure-skate and free-skate, and you'll very rarely get to grips with the tits on the periphery.

Roller skates are cheaper, but there aren't the rinks of yore. When will someone be bold enough to introduce the Roller Game or Derby to this country? Huge teams of women on roller-skates, smashing each other to pulp, and hurling one another into the congregation as they circle the track. *Rollerball* was not that fictitious.

Do-it-yourself Rink

I can remember at school, we made our own skating rink one year from thick snow on the House's tatty grass tennis court. We rolled the snow, having candle-greased the roller, and then at night, sprayed the result with water. By morning it was a crude ice rink. Those who could skate were able to, around the patches of grass that appeared here and there, but it wasn't an entirely unsuccessful venture.

CLEAN-VESTED INTERESTS

GYMNASTICS

Blame my Public School education if you like, God knows that however hard you fight to shed the advantages accrued, there are bound to be bits of shrapnel here and there in the body that play up in colder weather. Long-forgotten memories bound suddenly and uninvited into the system, as may the sharp whiff of plastic daffodils cause you to start suddenly and shudder for a reason you wot not of. So show me a gymnasium and I think at once of grubby mackintoshes. Perhaps, doctor, there still lurk in the murkier grey cells at the back, traces of adolescent fantasies and grubby jokes about knicker elastic and gym-slips. Maybe under hypnosis I might blurt out what occurred behind the gym, that causes me to feel unclean and a trifle tacky when admiring the antics of a fragile, flat-chested girl-child, be it a Korbet or a Comaneci. The television seems to fog and blur as the glass did years ago as my steamy breath blocked out the pubescent, white-armed Nausicaas romping within. A cold flannel, doctor? Nurse, the screens! Oh, Ava, you got to Trent Bridge just in time.

It is recommended by the British Amateur Gymnastics Association that if you wish to compete at the highest level (no, not swinging from the chandeliers), it is best if you are an eight-year-old girl. Even if you are, dear, 10 years from now you'll be well past it. Look at poor Olga, 21 and fit only for displays of geriatrics. Our source said seemingly sensibly that he doesn't like girls to get too serious too early. (Isn't this awfully true of life outside the gymnasium? But enough.) The danger, he maintained, is that if they do become too deeply steeped, they can become morons. They lose their personality and individuality, he vouchsafed, and then pointed to the Russians and the East Germans, not to mention Nadia Comaneci. Now you might think that perhaps our friend keeps in trim by running on the spot in a vat packed with sour grapes, treading out a fairly typical undrinkable British light table wine. Conversely, you might say that if we British are to hold our heads high again in gymnastical circles, leaps and heaves, we should have our girls, like Comaneci, at it 24 hours a day, and wipe the smile off *their* tiny, shining faces. What you can't do is have it both ways, and while I would prefer to think that Nadia under the mask of studied indifference is giggling and whooping like the kid she is, I am prepared to accept she may be the tight-lipped winner she appears. We appear to be a race of tight-lipped losers. Where is the English gymnast who will come a laughing sixty-third, finally landing one-handed on a

judge's head, politely asking for a light for their cheroot. Everyone loves a good loser, let us become brilliant at it.

Waxing philosophical our man at B.A.G.A. suggested that the popularity of gymnastics today springs from the world's search in the midst of increasing violence, guerrillas and rugby, hi-jackers and soccer, for some sport that is not only non-violent but aesthetically pleasing. (When I was in the Army our P.T.I. corporal was put away for emasculating an aircraftsman with his boot, but I take the B.A.G.A.'s point.)

Joining a club will cost about £1 per annum, and perhaps a further 10p a session. Find one affiliated to B.A.G.A. as they insist on a qualified coach being present and that is no bad thing. Although they swear purblind that most injuries are muscular, and none too serious at that, a lurking coach means you needn't wear a crash-helmet when approaching the springboard.

All you need to wear to start with is shorts and a T-shirt. In competition, of course, the girls wear leotards and the lads vests and shorts or long trousers, if bandy.

Acrobatics

There is a new branch sprouting – a mixture of circus acrobatics and gymnastics. If you've always been a dab hand at somersaults and hand-stands try this one. You get to balance ladies on your shoulders, lads, and throw them carelessly about. Or each other. My introduction to this aspect of the gym was on television when I saw two Russian gentlemen performing, as I saw it, the simple tale of two muscle-bound lovers discharged from the Moscow Circus for unnatural practices. They transpired to be two Vladimirs, and well known for that sort of thing. All this could be yours, dear. I felt it needed more of the circus – hands raised to all sides of the congregation, much bowing and cries of 'Hi' and infinitely more drum-rolls for effect.

Modern Rhythmic Gymnastics

This is up and coming as well, and I encountered it first shortly after falling upon the two Vladimirs. There was a lady gracefully doing inferior lasso-tricks with several yards of red tape and very little gymnastics. They can apparently do the same sort of thing with hoops and balls. It is for the older lady gymnast of 16 and upwards.

For information of Clubs, Hoops, Balls, etc. *British Amateur Gymnastics Association, 23a High Street, Slough, Bucks.*

TRAMPOLINING

Another thought while you're in your vest and pants and itching for action. Your nearest sports centre will doubtless run a course and provide a coach. There is an annual summer

school at Crystal Palace in August at about £40 a week.

There is a *British Trampoline Federation, 152a College Road, Harrow, Middlesex,* but no clubs as such as yet. The same vest and pants will suffice, but beginners are advised to cover their arms and legs for obvious reasons.

ATHLETICS

Despite the variety of sporting opportunities offered under this heading – running any number of distances, jumping up and over things, or off and into distant sandpits, running and jumping at the same time over hurdles or water-jumps, vaulting, throwing a rich collection of objects from javelins to hammers, walking yet – it may strike you as a mite churlish for me to confess that although I've tried all these activities once, always admittedly under duress, I would sooner thrust my best leg into a bag of piranha than participate again. Even spectating is a source of some pain if red, white and blue corpuscles still wrestle in your hardening arteries. I sit glued to Olympic Games. I first rented a colour set to capture the full flavour of Mexico City. And, oh but it's sad every four years to see so much hope evaporate, so many of our brightest hopes. Perhaps it's the foreign food, the change of diet, the water. In Mexico we blamed the altitude, in Munich the sudden descent to sea-level, in Montreal 'something was wrong in the Village', and the Russians were cheating and the Finns were having their blood changed every lap. And I blame the meat-rationing after the War again and . . . and it's high time again we looked at the whole structure of British athletics – again.

Like everything today it all boils down to lack of money. Apart from the obvious disadvantage of being stuck with the noble ideal of upholding the amateur principle against all odds and sods and the general run of the play in most other parts of the globe, the poor old Amateur Athletics Association as a structure is roofless, without electricity, full of rising damp and squatters, and should have been condemned years ago. It doesn't help in any way that the set-up is regionalised and that the three regions are stronger than the central body, and jealousy guard the prestige and rights of Number One. The proceeds of international meetings for instance are split in several directions, and swell no one's coffers. There's barely enough to feed Geoff Capes. The officials are honorary which means that those with any flair and expertise will be at best part-time. Being possessed of flair and expertise they'll be in high demand elsewhere. Some

are very good, and give much time and energy to the A.A.A., but there is a considerable amount of dead wood, which given the rotten state of the affair and the activities of the lesser stop-watch beetle, tends to fall heavily on the heads of the more talented.

Apart from which there's nothing the media enjoy more than fanning the flames of division between the A.A.A. and the athletes. This stems directly from the A.A.A.'s steadfast refusal to pay the athletes anything more than their precise expenses, so that the only way the athlete can pick up a bit on the side is by revealing all about the appalling state of British athletics, shock, horror, and could I have my small brown envelope now please?

Unlike the Iron Curtain countries we do not give away commissions in the Royal Corps of Shot Putters or the Brigade of Household Long Jumpers. Unlike America we don't give away sporting scholarships to universities, like for instance Kent, Ohio, where there is a three-year course in the Morse Code, allowing a student to mull quietly over the dots and dashes while churning round and round the track in pursuit of the ultimate Gold. We also lack as a nation the necessary fanaticism and dedication and we view those who have it with great suspicion. When Brian Close, for instance, made his famous 70 for England, dancing down the wicket to Hall and Griffith, taking bouncers on the head and never showing the slightest wince, he didn't play for his county again for three years. Not sporting, what? The Americans enjoy successes in whatever field, in more ways than one, and in Russia you can wind up a Grand Master of the Hammer, with a colonel's pips and a brand-new penthouse overlooking the Kremlin.

You don't have to be amateurish to be amateurs. Given the success of Brendan Foster and Gateshead and Alan Pascoe's efforts at Crystal Palace, I would have thought there was a powerful case for workers' control. It would probably be the making of British sport. Nationalise it, hand the Ministry over to Tony Benn, if he's still free. If in your locality there's a football ground, a park or two, a greyhound track, a racecourse perhaps, that's an amazing amount of open space, lying fallow for quite long periods, and all under separate managements. Ram them all under the same aegis and now you have some local facilities to play with. Then start whipping up local pride and local heroes. Improve the catering, for God's sake, it is vile at most sporting occasions. Sort out the parking, use your local radio and press and woo your public back, not only to spectate, but to participate.

Involve the sportsmen and women too. The situation at the moment is not unlike the snarl-up of London's traffic, where the last people ever asked for advice, if at all, are the breed who live in it and work in it, indeed are up to here in it – the taxi drivers. Sportspersons too tend to be treated like errant children. It's no wonder they become petulant and sulk and refuse to play in your yard. Put *them* on the boards and committees and pay them director's fees. Give Geoff Capes, for instance, his enormous dinners in the executive dining rooms, the tab picked up by a grateful nation. This is one way round keeping our athletes happy financially, the other is to borrow the brilliant device of a famous U.S. sprinter, some 30 years ago or so, who would play poker all night with his sponsor and by some strange quirk never fail to win a sum not unakin to the sort of sum they might have paid him, but for . . . etc.

Well, thank Gawd, that's over and an answer has finally been found. I must go and lie down.

One rumour circulating athletics now for many years must be quashed and that is that

the Greeks and their Olympic Games were the start of it all. Not at all, although their sporting version of the martial arts current at the time, spear-throwing, Army-issue discus-hurling, wrestling, swimming and running like hell, has always been viewed as the start of competitive athletics, that was in fact 600 years earlier than the first Olympiad in 1829 B.C. at the Tailtin Games in Ireland. If you study *The Book of Leinster*, no shelf is complete without it, you will find that stone-putting and hammer throwing, Roth Cleas or the

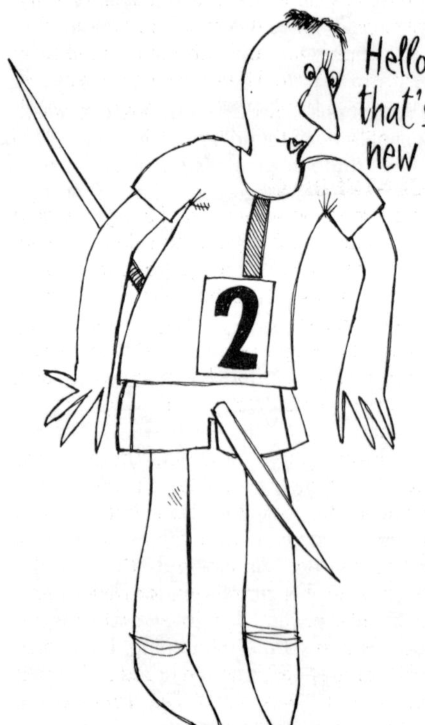

Wheel Feat were the crowd pullers in those days. I suppose that if it became common knowledge that the Irish began it all, it would play merry hell with the Olympic Code and the hopes and dreams of the late Baron Pierre de Coubertin. Incidentally, Henry VIII was no slouch at 'casting the bar', or hammer throwing.

The advantage of taking up athletics and joining a club, is that there will be something there for you somewhere on track or in field. If you simply want to run, you will quickly find your distance, it can be anything from 100 yards to the Marathon. At the same time a coach may see in your sprinting style that God in his wisdom in fact designed you for the hop, step and jump. Something in your bearing at the bar may else betray a bent for the pole vault. Now take Geoff Capes for instance, who I admit is a hero of mine – if I'd eaten my greens as Granny told me and still stuffed half an ox down me daily I could have been like him. His life is not all spent solitary in the semi-circle putting the shot. He lifts weights, runs, jumps, eats and otherwise mingles in athleticism at large. There seems to be a cheery camaradie amongst athletes themselves. If only it spread to the office block.

ORIENTEERING

This is becoming something of a rage. I blame Christopher Brasher, the horseless steeple-chaser that was. In honesty, it appears not to be as brutish as I thought at first. I thought it consisted solely of sprinting cross-country through the Pilgrim's Progress with only a despondent A-Z of Slough to bring you solace, a sport designed for clean-living militant Christians.

On investigation, however, there seems more to it. At international level it is survival of the fittest, not only the fittest but an even rarer breed who can also read intelligently on the trot through unknown terrain. In the broader view, it is car-rallying for pedestrians. The Swedes invented it to alleviate the intensely boring nature of running. I can only run 50 yards at best, and am bored stiff in that short time. If I was doing *The Times* crossword, however, at the same time, I would be

arse over elbow in the first five feet, but interested and amused. That is orienteering. Armed with a map, a compass and a list of control points, the competitors set off at one-minute intervals into the unknown, and unknown it is. Not only is the course a total secret until the start, but its very location also is until as late as possible. It is quite often composed under the guise of a NATO operation or such. So bang goes the obvious device of having your family, the more elderly, the children, line some part of the fast lane, to wave Swedish flags, shout encouragement and point vigorously in quite the wrong direction. Better that they enter. It is an ideal occupation for both hare and tortoise.

To this end, competitors are offered a choice of routes, th classic alternative is 'over or round', and whil the young and virile can pick a swift belt down a sheep-track for a mile, some of us may well prefer to make our own way less actively to the same objective through a couple of hundred yards of light jungle. The speediest mind wins. The experts consult their maps every two seconds while moving at pace. One move in the wrong direction and you're doomed. The forests echo with the distant cries of failed orienteers.

There are about 100 clubs in Britain now who provide instruction and there's an event somewhere virtually every weekend. It's brilliantly organised, simply ring the National Office in Nottinghamshire, Dethick 628, and they will tell you where to go. The only expense is getting there, and your club will doubtless organise a lift.

British Orienteering Federation, 14 Glenochil Road, Falkirk, Stirlingshire, FK1 5LT.

WEIGHT LIFTING

Not, as you might at first imagine, a sport only for Central European giants or Russians built like a beef mountain, lack of stature can apparently be of some advantage, short-arse, and no hindrance whatsoever. Look at 'Precious' Mackenzie, for instance. It's simply that, like boxing, the heavies get the coverage. As in life again, as well.

Sheer strength and brute force though are not enough. You need speed, coordination, skill and a special pair of boots. Thus equipped, however, and you're away. You need a firm grasp of the basics, not to mention the dumbbells, these can be grasped at a club, or in some parts, evening classes. (List from *British Amateur Weightlifting Association, 3 Iffley Turn, Oxford.*)

It's cheap. Club membership is as little as £1 a year, and 15p for an evening's workout. Only when you near the top will you need the tracksuit, the bathing costume, the elastic knee-caps, the athletic support and the surgical belt, otherwise it's simply a question of getting out there and picking the bloody things up.

Olympic Lifting

This is the one for you, dear. We'll have you rubbing your vast shoulders with the great.

Olympic lifting is not to be confused with power lifting, which is simply a test of strength, and very popular in borstals where it burns up surplus energy. That is more for the body-builder. For the Olympics you must master the snatch and the jerk, which sounds like a chapter in an American sex manual.

You'll recognise them when you see them.

A major part of the sport would seem to be the animal pacing about, the snorting and blowing, the butch application of talcum powder, the roaring as you tackle the bell-bar. Work on these in private, and startle a neighbour.

The major expense would seem to be food. Pounds of steak are needed to cultivate the necessary body. Eat a Russian, probably a deal tastier than a Peruvian fly-half.

SUBLIMATED VIOLENCE
If you are of a violent disposition and soccer hooliganism is not enough, and you are too squeamish perhaps to hunt the beasts of the field or blast the birds out of the air, though I suspect your dog is no stranger to your boot when your aggressions are flying low, perhaps kicking the shit out of your fellow-man may attract. Again, football offers openings and we shall come to boxing and croquet in the foulness of time but in the meantime what of wrestling or even better, as heavily advertised, the marital arts. (That is a knowing misprint and should read martial arts. Am I not a wag?)

WRESTLING
We shall ignore professional wrestling though the pressures of remembering the script while in the grip of a Triple-Buttock or whatever, must provide the equivalent brain-strain to orienteering.

There are our own ancient forms like Cumberland or Westmoreland, which looks not unlike a two-man ball-less rugby scrum at work, but in the Olympics they plump for freestyle or Greco-Roman. Greco-Roman is freestyle except you can't use your legs, or his. I suppose the Greeks or Romans were frequently legless, they trained exclusively on Retsina and Chianti.

J. Ross, the Honourable Secretary of the *British Amateur Wrestling Association, 13 Kay Park Terrace, Kilmarnock, KA3 7AZ* will give any information on clubs to join. The membership fees are minimal, and so is the kit. Swimming trunks and gym shoes are the basics, though for bouts, wrestling not drinking, a red or blue one-piece costume is worn, probably for easier identification afterwards.

JUDO
This may seem a bit old hat now that everyone else is into karate, aikido and the occasional kendo. And whatever happened to baritsu, or Japanese wrestling, of which Sherlock Holmes claimed to be a master, prior to falling off the Reichenbach Falls? It's all about, as they say in commentating circles, 'nagewaza-ing' and

'katamewaza-ing'. Throwing and holding. The better you are, the more 'ippons" you get, or points. What pretty names. If you fail to make an 'ippon' you can be awarded a 'waza-ari' which, to listen to, I think I would prefer. There are two waza-aris to one ippon, though with the Japanese economy as it is today, heaven knows where it will all end. Even the penalties sound like the tinkling music of the geisha, as the tiny creature rolls bonzai logs across the ornamental pond. In increasing order of gravity they range from the shido, the chui, the keikoku to the hausoko-make, which means an early bath, a rare delight I would have thought as in that happy land the bathing is mixed, and the little ladies trip up and down your back on their little feet.

Apart from anything else, the costume itself, the judogi, makes excellent bed-wear. They cost £5-£10, and as they are reinforced in the more necessary places, last well.

There are over 1000 clubs under the auspice of the *British Judo Association, 70 Brompton Road, London, SW3 1EX*, and these quote quite a wide range of fees.

THE MARTIAL ARTS

Now we're into kendo, karate, aikido, kung fu and the Korean variations. The post-mortem revealed that Bruce Lee was a fearsome mess within as a result of excessive kung fu, so be warned. A further warning, a B.B.C. person told this story against himself, through clenched teeth. He was in a pub when another custo-

mer became belligerent, and was clearly looking for a fracas. 'Take care', said the B.B.C., and pointed out, in all honesty, that he was a Black Belt in karate. Those were the last words he remembered uttering until he woke up in hospital three days later, having suffered a vigorous kneeing.

There is now a *Martial Arts Commission* at *6/16 Deptford Bridge, London, SE9 4JS* (Nos. 8-14 were destroyed in a fit of pique by a former secretary. I lie.) – to impress upon the young the deadly nature of the sports, and keep them off the streets and back in the gymnasia or Hong Kong Film Studios where they belong. They were conceived originally by Nippon priests who got round the vow of non-violence, by forswearing weapons, but decapitating brigands with a swift back-hander. It's all very well to know your kung fu-crazy son is in the right hands, but alarming to know in your heart he can sever a pile of bricks with his left. Still, the danger is impressed upon all who take up the Arts, and the Japanese virtues of self-control and hat-raising are also included in the training. Nevertheless, remember Pearl Harbour.

The difference between karate and aikido is that karate is a straight fight, although they pull punches, kicks, etc., whereas aikido is defender versus attacker, sometimes with one of the parties armed with a rubber knife.

Kendo is more up my alley, but only because it looks most impressive. Fine armour, and judges who pronounce in semaphore by waving flags. They beat each other about with long bamboo poles called 'shinai', and as in all the martial arts there is plenty of jumping in the air and guttural squawking. Why not?

There are above 800 karate clubs in Great Britain – £3 per annum and about 50p an evening. The kit (gi) similar to Judo kit costs about £8.

OUR FATHER...
AMEN...
AH SO!

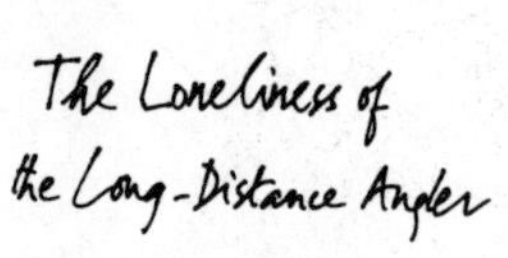

THE CARP BAGGERS

FISHING

If you're not an aficionado, pun half-intended, you may not realise that fame and fortune can be won in the fields of fishing. There are countless competitions to be won. In match fishing you can win £5000 a year, though admittedly much of that is from backing yourself with the bookies. There is international fishing yet, hence the Cod War, the Cod Peace and delightful medals to be won.

England have never, in fact, won the World Championships, but they sound action-packed. I quote:

'There have been other massacres of the same magnitude over the years, and there can be no doubt that local knowledge of the water contributed greatly to Italy's triumph. They knew that at times it was possible to feed with vast quantities of maggots, choking up the tiny bleak *(pronounced bleak: a fish that chokes apparently)*. The Italians' feeding staggered English observers. Each man laced in six gallons of maggots as loose feed in the three hours. No water in Britain would take such a hammering over five hours, let alone three.' *(Woodbine Angling Yearbook 1972.)*

One imagines the terraces went wild, and yet you never hear of fishing violence, unless you're a fish.

The National Championship is the big one for the match angler with Team Contest and an Individual Title. That title is something of a long-shot, such is the size of the entry, and depends a lot on the luck of the draw, meaning where you're sat. Only one gentleman, a fine looking gentleman with waxed moustaches like unfriendly-sword-fish, Jim Bazely, ever won it twice, once in 1909 and then not again

until 1927. We've had a couple of World Champions, though, the last in 1971 Robin Harris who got an M.B.E. as well.

Like so many sports we are deeply admired as individuals, but viewed as dumb-bells when it comes to teamwork. Selection committees again.

What sort of man is it, you must ask yourself prior to joining their ranks, who will sit on a river-bank in all weathers under a green umbrella, occasionally perhaps catching a fish, only to have to throw it back again? That's me, you may say, in one. Very well then, join a club, which considerably cuts the cost, even if you do have to tramp, grasping your tackle, some miles along the river-bank to find the club-patch. Fishing must be, apart from golf and war, the most popular sport for misogynists and for those who hate children with the intensity of W. C. Fields. And yet, there's peace and quiet, and in these brain-bending days, peace and quiet tastes better than fish.

SALMON FISHING

This is the fishing referred to in Huntin', Shootin' and Fishin'.

It costs a small fortune. You can find the odd package which for accommodation, fishing, food, rods, tuition, etc. costs in the region of £250 per week.

Firms occasionally seek to seduce foreign businessmen in this manner. Simply to fish on a stretch of good river for a week can cost you £75. You can get a fortnight in Majorca for that, with no fear of being savaged by infuriated salmon.

Cost:

A salmon-fishing rod, reel, etc.	£110
Kit – waders, daft hat, etc.	£50
Landing nets, register book, etc.	£40
	£200

You will also need a priest. This is a salmon-bludgeon, so called as it administers the last rites. It is this sort of callous humour that causes the most pain to fish. And they're said to be good for the brain.

A useful book to have to hand is D. A. Orton's *Where To Fish*, (*see Bibliography*). This comes out annually and tells you what to catch, where to catch it, the cost of catching it, and whether it was legal to catch it or not.

The National Anglers Council, 5 Cowgate, Peterborough, Cambs., will give you more information.

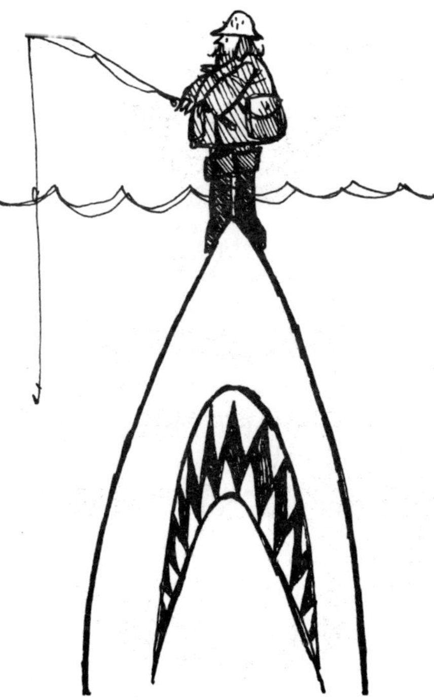

IT CAME FROM BEYOND THE BOTTOM OF THE DEEP
I INTEND TO SAVE THE WORLD WITH A COCKTAIL OF MAGGOT, WORM, AND A LITTLE CASTER
MY HERO!

SEA ANGLING

This is for the man who needs an even greater distance between himself and his home-comforts. (However, his wife has a fridge full of bait to remind her of him, a touching memento for her to wallow in, as far as he's concerned.) You operate from the beach or from a boat, the major expense, some £40, though club membership will lessen that considerably. Even so, it'll be about £10 for a day's fishing for boat and bait, etc. A bloke to whom we spoke reckons the fish he's caught over the years work out at £3 an ounce. 'What of your wife?' we enquired. I'm not sùre where all this concern started, but it betrays a heart. 'Good game!' he cried, chuckling rudely. 'Out all night. Not a bite. And nobody knows where you've been.' It sounded like the chorus of a song. It may well be, sung late at night on lonely beaches or indeed the Station Hotel, Ramsgate.

The National Federation of Sea Anglers will reveal all from their premises at *26 Downsview Crescent, Uckfield, East Sussex.* You can be drummed out of the Federation for selling your catch. You are, however, allowed to eat what there is of it, and much of what there is is inedible.

SHARK

They sought it with thimbles, they sought it with care
They pursued it with forks and hope,
They threatened its life with a railway-share;
They charmed it with smiles and soap.'

LEWIS CARROLL

For this sport you will need a beaver, a butcher and above all else a bellman. Maps are unnecessary, preferred is 'a perfect and absolute blank'. I appear to have gone mad. It's my writing. I could have sworn I wrote 'Snark'. Start again.

SNARK

I don't think many Britons gave much thought to shark until *Jaws*. Even then I thought the film might fall flat on its face here, as it touched on a fear few of us feel. Australians on the other hand never venture onto a beach without shark repellent in their tucker-bags. Coastal Americans too know precisely what the movie was hinting at.

Toby was given a strange game for Christmas called *Maneater* which gives him constant joy. Four swimmers set off across the board towards a distant beach, losing points and

legs on the way to a rather smug looking shark piece. Sharks have arrived definitely.

The Shark Angling Club of Great Britain, The Quay, East Looe, Cornwall, will tell you where best and how to set about them in those parts. Cornwall is our longest-established shark hunting area. You can't join the Club in fact until you have caught one over 75 pounds. This will cost you £2.25 entrance fee and £3 a year thereafter.

What you may well ask, showing perhaps my repeated fear of dead horses, do you do if lumbered with 75 pounds or so of solid shark, yet another embarrassment about the home. Have no fear, once weighed it vanishes to become bait, the fins soup-wards.

(A small tip. If you do catch one, don't drag it up the beach tail-first, it will bring up its all, bait and rubby-dubby, and consequently lose weight. It would be foolish to lose your chance of membership for a load of old rubby-dubby.)

What is rubby-dubby? Pardon me while I down an overdose of Entero-Vioform. Rubby-dubby is a light *bouillabaisse* of fish heads and fish guts crammed into several bags, with small holes cut in them to allow a steady seep as you tow them behind you creating a 'smell lane' – extremely attractive to a gourmet shark. Using rubby-dubby is 'chumming', which is bloody silly when contemplated. All good stuff to know though, the essence of fishing is lying in your teeth, and that sort of knowledge pads out the mendacity no end.

I can recommend Brigadier J. A. L. Caunter's book *Shark Angling in Great Britain* (*see Bibliography*) to all those who have no intention of fishing for shark, but would like to give the impression they have.

'Shark', he says, 'are catholic in their taste'. Incidentally, you're more likely to lose a leg via a shark in the afternoon.

'One might postulate', postulates the Brigadier, 'with justification, I think, that the better the boatman is at using "rubby-dubby", the better the sport – other things being equal, of course'. Of course.

THE HUNTING OF SHARK

Go to Cornwall and pay for an excursion. You'll get the kit thrown in, and advice from the boatman. As to how to get the kit out again, for instance. There are more sophisticated boats with executive-style swivel chairs, and less without. The hire of a boat in Looe, Cornwall, is £36 (kit and bait inclusive), and it will house four anglers. About 20 boats go out daily from Looe – seven days a week.

'Tagging a shark', says the Brigadier, 'even a small one is not free of risk, and should a slashed hand or arm be suffered it might have serious consequences for the boatman concerned'.

There are only four clubs affiliated to the *Shark Angling Club of Great Britain.* All enquiries, except concerning accommodation, to *The Secretary, Brian Tudor, East Looe, Cornwall.*

Balls
My
Liege

BALL

THE INEVITABLE

It's amazing that we've got this far without one. Think sport and you see them everywhere, we roll them, lob them, serve them, receive them, hit them with a rare variety of items, miss them, throw them at each other's heads, play the man instead of them and roar with laughter at the hoariest *double-entendres* concerning them every time it's dropped in a changing room, which is as often as trousers. There's the happy tale of a civil servant receiving one of those circulars that circulate a Ministry and, being asked to pencil in his comments prior to passing it on, to avoid writing 'Balls' boldly, wrote 'Round objects'. A superior, on seeing this, enquired loftily, 'Who is this Round, and to what does he object?'

The point is with ball-games, that you either have an eye for one or not. If not, I for one think none the less of you. You, in your turn, probably don't drown as often as I do, and can understand VAT.

The Evolution of the Ball Game

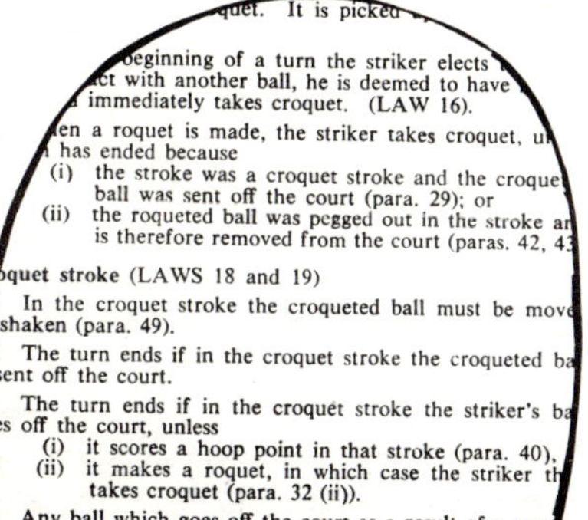

quet. It is picked

beginning of a turn the striker elects
ct with another ball, he is deemed to have
immediately takes croquet. (LAW 16).

en a roquet is made, the striker takes croquet, u
has ended because
(i) the stroke was a croquet stroke and the croque
ball was sent off the court (para. 29); or
(ii) the roqueted ball was pegged out in the stroke a
is therefore removed from the court (paras. 42, 4

oquet stroke (LAWS 18 and 19)

. In the croquet stroke the croqueted ball must be mov
shaken (para. 49).

9. The turn ends if in the croquet stroke the croqueted b
s sent off the court.

0. The turn ends if in the croquet stroke the striker's b
goes off the court, unless
(i) it scores a hoop point in that stroke (para. 40),
(ii) it makes a roquet, in which case the striker t
takes croquet (para. 32 (ii)).

1. Any ball which goes off the court as a result of a cro
roke is replaced on the yard-line at the point neare
ere it went off. (LAW 8).

uation Stroke (LAW 20)
fter the croquet stroke the striker plays a con

turn has ended under para. 29 or 3
roquet, in which

ROLLERBALL

CROQUET

Reputed to be one of the most vicious sports on earth, it is however a very pretty game. It is written into the Rules for instance that if black and blue balls versus red and yellow offends your eye, clashes with your herbaceous border or by the very colours reminds you of an unpleasant incident at an Annual General Meeting of the M.C.C., you can play brown and green against pink and white. To watch them play the Hurlingham Club is to be transported back to the gracious days of the

See the genial gentlefolk play at a friendly game of Croquet,
Watch the endless hocus-pocus 'midst the daisy and the crocus!
Croquet Rules, O.K.?
OH, THE CROQUET-ROQUET
OH, THE CROQUET-ROQUET
OH THE CROQUET-ROQUET

With Mallet Aforethought

Crimean War. Blazered gentry and their long-frocked ladies sit sipping tea in small striped tents while battle rages beneath them. The death-rate is slightly less, of course, than that of the 17th Lancers, but the ambiance is strikingly similar. Close your eyes and you can hear the crack and whistle of heavy ball, the thud of mallets against bone, the whinnying of dying horses, the battle-cries and oaths of old soldiers at play.

The Croquet Association operate from the *Hurlingham Club* itself, *London, SW6* and will point you at one of the 70 or so affiliated clubs, but if you're blessed with a lawn, of course, grab yourself a coffin-like box of mallets, hoops, balls, etc. and do it yourself. Sets cost between £35 and £55. I would suggest that if you wish to pursue croquet seriously you seek out someone who's played it to take you over the course first. A brief thumb through the Rules has left me a little wiser and a deal older. They would be a boon and blessing to W. S. Gilbert had he survived, but then again perhaps it was his efforts to interpret them that laid that great man finally low, face-to-face with the terminal hoop. He probably suffered a continuation stroke (*see Rule 20*).

BOWLS

I suppose I was 17 when I first admitted to myself that I would never sport for England, and, as I remember, it was then that I conceived the excellent notion of taking up bowls, working on the theory that I had 40 years to reach international standard, but that having a good head's start on the rest of the field, I should walk it. That was 23 years ago and to date I haven't done a thing about it. I have only myself to blame, and yet another boat I've missed hoots mockingly as it vanishes around the point. Anyway, as in all sport today the competition is more intense, and they say only one in a thousand makes it to international level. A word of cheer, however, it *is* possible to reach that level in five years.

Lawn Bowls is the one you probably see more often from the top of the bus, although Crown Bowls enjoys great popularity in the North of England. Should the conductor ask you in that enchanting sing-song accent that evokes the sun, the distant palm trees, the cheery music of the dustbin bands, the gay Calypso of his island home, which is being played, the difference is easily spottable. Lawn

Bowls is played by gentlemen in white panamas, multi-badged blazers and white flannels and ladies in white box-pleated skirts and ungainly hats from one end of a rectangular lawn to the other. Crown Bowls is played on a grassy square, higher at the centre than at the edges, by men in sensible caps.

There is also quite a lot of indoor bowls, easily recognisable from the top of every bus, and a sound idea in our uncertain clime.

The joy of bowls is that you can start playing at eight and continue virtually uninterrupted for the rest of your life. If is not as sedate as it looks, I've seen frail old men dance and leap after their wood, like Kevin Keegan after a goal, urging, cajoling and praying it to lie adjacent to the jack. They cover a fair distance in an afternoon.

Useful Addresses

English Indoor Bowling Association, 730 Romford Road, London, E.12.

English Bowling Association, 4 Lansdowne Crescent, Bournemouth, BH1 1RX.

British Crown Green Amateur Bowling Association, 21 Beechwood Road, Bedworth, Nuneaton, Warwicks.

English Women's Bowling Federation, 'Devonia', 305 Dogsthorpe Road, Peterborough, Cambs.

English Women's Indoor Bowling Association, 'Brendon', 63 Forlease Road, Maidenhead, Berks.

TEN-PIN BOWLING

This appears to be fast dying in Britain, and no bad thing. The Bowling Alley and the Bingo Hall are two of our greatest post-War ecological blots. Where there used to be over 1000 lanes, there are now less than half. You may feel therefore that your chances of honours are considerably enhanced, and I shan't try to dissuade you. The first time I played I dislocated a finger, and spent all evening watching my ball ricochet down the gutters, or hitting a bar that kept being lowered between myself and the skittles. The computers were never troubled. The second time was a charitable match between *That Was The Week That Was* and a gang of scrawny models. The main excitement was being teamed with Peter O'Toole (*see Index under Name Dropping*) who insisted on bowling over-arm. This revolutionary technique, though extremely successful, was frowned upon as it caused dents in the track. It wreaked merry havoc however among the pins and the computer, I am happy to report, had a seizure.

There are World Championships annually, and if you are prepared, as the British team is, to train for 15-20 hours a week (3 hours a night, every night!) in those soul-less canyons, surrounded by appalling noise and clatter, you could find yourself in the unlikeliest of places and mingling with a most respectable class of person. At a recent World Championship in Teheran, under the auspice of the Shah, or vice versa, under the Shah of auspice, you would have competed with doctors, lawyers, accountants, asset-strippers and a dolphin-trainer. Not the sort of person you

would expect to meet in a British bowling alley, but then if you've ever needed the professional services of any of the above, you will know that they are invariably playing golf.

If you must indulge in this boring, noisy sport contact *The British Ten-Pin Bowling Association, 19 Canterbury Avenue, Ilford, Essex,* and they will tell you what alleys still remain.

BOULES

This is to lawn bowls as cyclo-cross is to bicycling, and while we're into games that basically involve rolling balls at one another, I would commend this to you. You may not know where your nearest bowling green is, but drive into some French town or village when the *boules* is afoot, and you'll know where the action is. Bunting and bands, of which the world needs more daily, abound, and in the midst of a cheering, wine-stained assembly are the Frenchest of Frenchmen hurling the metal *boules* out of the backs of their hands towards the squatting jack. The roar as the *boule* bites into the gravel, stopping at once in its tracks smack on the jack, or cracks like a rifle-shot into the opponent's *boule* sending it whistling into the distance, fills the air with the pungent aroma of rogue garlic. I never travel to France without my battered *boule.* It's a bit like taking cannonballs to Waterloo, but you get instant respect as the owner of your own personal pitted lump.

You can play it literally anywhere. (The flat below may complain, but there is also a small indoor version available.) Gravel with concrete beneath is best, but you'll find that outside any decent hotel. Anyway, it's worth looking, isn't it? It gives a holiday to France a sense of purpose.

MARBLES

The most famous marbles are, of course, the Elgin Marbles, but this has nothing to do with it. I wish it had. There are always those who will say that there is no room for politics in sport, in itself a rude blow below the belt for the Minister of it. These are the same people who will refuse to believe that there is politics in *anything* and have upped the drawbridge,

battened down the hatches, closed shutters, eyes and ears, blocked out the sun, narrowed their minds and only emerge every now and then blinking against the light to vote Conservative like Granny always did.

Of course, sport is politics, and vice versa, but to a lesser extent. Every decision reached by any national or international sporting body is political, be it the M.C.C., the Football League, the Football Association, the German Democratic Republic Deltoid Manufacturing Company, the New Zealand Rugby Union (the All-Blackshirts), and Chilean Football Association (more behind barbed wire on the pitch than off it), the Chinese Ping-Pong team, or the Russian Radio-Controlled Sabre Company Limited. It's all politics.

Take some seemingly straightforward occasion such as an amateur heavyweight boxing match between an American and a Russian. They are not, as the Olympic motto would have us believe, simply two large citizens of the world competing, with the best man winning, pigeons erupting from his corner at the conclusion, handshakes all round and cries of *'Vive le sport!'*. It's East versus West, Marxist versus Supermarket, Black versus White, a Captain in the Russian Army versus a Boxing Scholar to an American University who has just got a Ph.D. for writing a thesis on *The Stacking of Towels*. It's them against us or us against them, depending on which corner you happen to be sitting in.

The moment you have world championships, something appalling happens to the game. It becomes in peacetime the equivalent of the normal processes of war. Since the redundancy of diplomats, which came with the invention of the hot-line and Henry Kissinger, we no longer have diplomatic incidents, but we have equally nerve-wracking off-the-ball incidents that cause fingers to itch round the Red Button. We have dope-tests and sex-tests, and walk-outs and boycotts. All international politics.

What does it actually prove if you have the world marbles championship cup on the mantelpiece at Number Ten, or wherever they would house it? That to be a nation from whose loins has sprung the marbles champion of the world, proves to all others that your way of life is superior to any other, that a mixed economy works, that your weather is wonderful, your cuisine superb, that the Thatcher is not a dying breed? Not at all, though the fact that the papers are full of him, Frank Bough all over him, and he's awarded the M.B.E. may lead you to think otherwise.

Here sits Britain like a rancid old man on a park bench, rank and stiff with meths, shouting toothlessly at passers-by from under a pile of newspaper, 'I was Chairman of I.C.I., give us £5.83 for a mug of tea, or I'll breathe on you'. Whether or not, we lead the world at marbles is irrelevant. It's positive proof of absolutely nil.

To wail as we do about the condition of British football, 'and we', they moan, 'who taught the whole world soccer'. Damned fools, we should have kept it to ourselves, as the Americans have so wisely done with grid-iron and baseball. They always win the world series, and feel a lot better for it.

Harold Wilson may well say, and I've heard him say it, that had England beaten West Germany in Mexico, the General Election that week would have gone his way. It wouldn't, and neither is our current parlous state anything to do with our general incompetence on the park.

Which brings me back to the Elgin Marbles, at the feet of which I should never have been

in the first place. Suffice to say that when I hear the stands ejaculate 'Eng-land! Eng-land!' before going off into some chauvinistic paroxysm I remind myself that they are shouting of the country, mine too I admit, that nicked the Marbles off the Greeks and won't give them back, thus forcing them to hold up a portion of the Acropolis with shoddy plastic replicas. It restores your sense of proportion.

Apart from which, if we did hand back all the stuff we looted, raped, borrowed, and purloined during the heady days of the Empire, the British Museum, thus denuded, would make a first-rate sports centre, unlike some. The Victoria and Albert Museum would make an excellent home for British marbles, and being but a short walk away for me, might set a whole new sporting life in motion.

Last Thoughts on the Elgin Marbles
What about putting them up as first prize in a game of football against Greece? This would add a dash of spice to the game. Duelling was at heart a sport, fighting over ladies' hands, and an excellent way to settle differences, with minimal casualties (all right, 50 per cent, but 50 per cent of very little), and the result was clear-cut and irreversible. Even so I can picture the British Duelling Association sitting up for any number of lunches debating as to whether 11 paces is more of a crowd-puller than 10.

How much more sensible to settle international arguments in the David versus Goliath manner. Choice of sport would, of course, be a stumbling block. For example, the Americans would have wiped out the Vietnamese at baseball but would quite clearly have lost all hands down against the wily Cong at orienteering. I would, if asked, have suggested a game of cricket, strange to both participants, with British umpires.

A Cheering Note
There has not been a war between any two cricketing nations since the Boer War, when they didn't play it, except for a recent encounter between India and Pakistan. There's a moral there somewhere. Keep politics out of sport, you will suggest, but then I suspect it was you who couldn't understand why World War II prevented our playing Germany at marbles in the summer of 1942.

MARBLES
A very cheap sport. The only equipment you need is a tolly (a shooting marble) which costs 30p. To join the *British Isles Marbles Association (Crawley Sports Centre, Haslett Avenue, Crawley, Sussex)* costs only 25p per annum. So for 55p you are on your way to the marbling hall of fame. One snag is that a team called the Toocan Terribles has won the British title 20 times in the last 22 years, but you will be happy to learn, they were recently beaten by the Pernod Rams. Where there's life, there's hope.

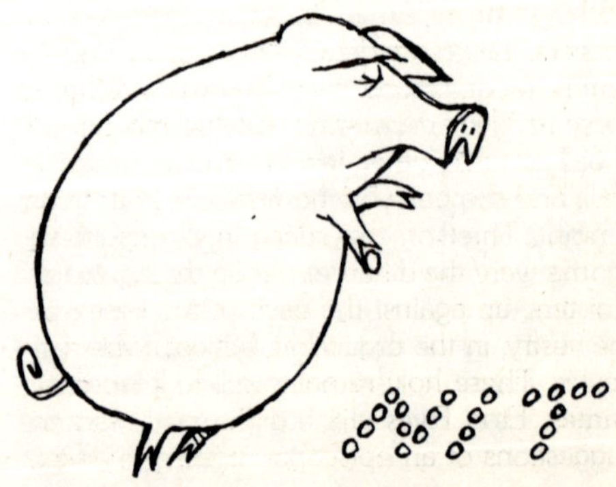

A KIND OF LOBBING

SQUASH (AND THE EVOLUTION OF BALL GAMES)

I've long maintained that I'm not so much a Revo, as an Evo, although I don't think I believe that anymore either. Evolutionaries have to be optimists, and I think were he alive today even Mr Micawber would be constantly on the telphone to the Samaritans. Even so, it's quite interesting to follow the natural course of ball-games (Εφαιpistiki* the Greeks had a word for it).

* Excuse failure here of Ancient Greek Type-writer

Jeux de palmes the French used to call them, which suggests blindness and stunted growth; they were content simply to throw a ball to and fro. Something of a Revo was when they discovered that by wearing gloves they could throw it harder and it hurt less. Some wag then stuck his glove on the end of a stick, inventing quite unknowingly, the primitive bat. This became a more sophisticated article with the coming of crude rackets. As I've pointed out before, monks have a lot to answer for, and armed with gloves and rackets and nothing much to do between matins and vespers, they created early versions of squash, tennis, racquets and fives. The rules of all of these revolve around two or so people hitting a ball at each other, either directly or via a wall, and the person who first misses it, loses a point. The only difference in the sports of monks were the different playing areas. In the cloisters, up against the back of the vestry, in the vestry, in the organ loft, between the gargoyles. These holy remains still lurk in some games. Eton Fives still has the buttress and suggestions of an episcopal drainage system,

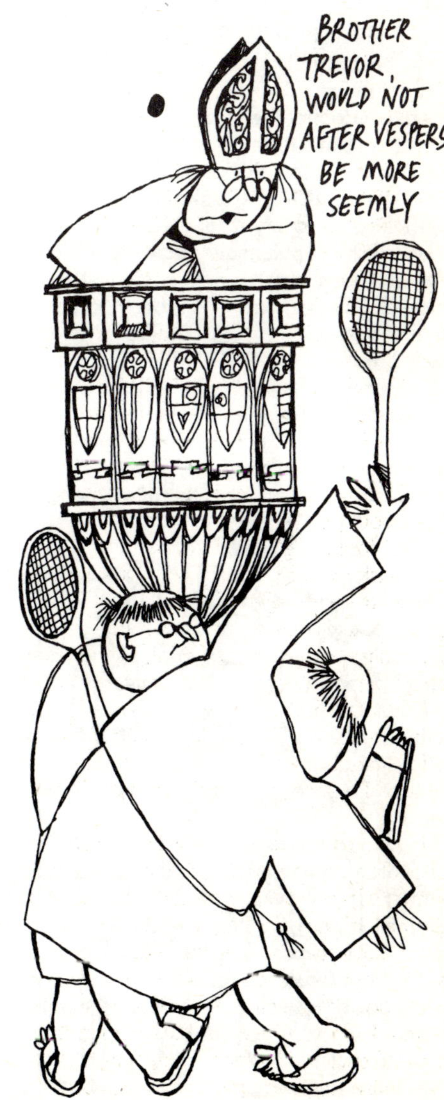

Real Tennis is clearly played in the back of someone's cathedral. Squash has none of these obstructions owing nothing to monks and, to my mind, is the more boring for it. There *is* a door at the back of the court which, if opened, can suddenly put a player off quite considerably, but this has now given way in many instances to a glass wall for spectators and television to pry through. It has become enormously popular, although I gave it up years ago after nearly suffering my first coronary at Dolphin Square. The score stood at 5-4 in the first game, as I remember, before passing out.

The origins of squash lie in (*a*) the Debtors' Prison at Newgate that was and (*b*) Harrow School where the rubber ball was introduced to save on broken windows. The latter in my view being precisely what the game needs.

However, it's undoubtedly popular, so popular that most clubs have lengthy waiting lists and even if accepted it's very difficult to find a vacant court. You quite often have to ring up a week in advance and could find yourself playing at 11 at night, which is no time for a coronary. Clubs also have matches, which occupy the courts further and they also seem embroiled in leagues and ladders. There you are, like it or not, on a ladder and you're then plagued by keen young opponents eager to knock you off, usually at about 10 in the morning. Not a good time for a coronary either.

In case you think I'm gelding the lilo slightly, perhaps overstating the case against squash, let me say at once that few stand higher in my estimation than Jonah Barrington. Also that apart from my feeling that as a game it is over-strenuous and leans towards the dull, let me add that it is very expensive.

Club subs can cost about £25 a year, plus a pound or so for necessary lighting each time you play. A list of clubs from the *Squash Rackets Association, 70 Brompton Road, London, SW3*, costs you 35p. There are about 2000 of them, perhaps it would be best to shop around and find the one with the happiest ratio of members and courts and which operate for the longest hours.

The kit, surprisingly, is quite reasonable. You can be clad and tooled up for £20.

RACQUETS

As only about 700 people in the country play racquets or if you like rackets, but the former spelling smacks less of the Mafiosa (and there are occasional matches against America), there would seem to be both more chance of getting a court and a fair chance of playing for England.

REAL TENNIS

'Let cricketers await the tardy sun
Break one another's shins and call it fun:
Let Scotia's golfers through the affrighted land
With crooked knee and glaring eyeball stand;
Let football rowdies show their straining thews,
And tell their triumphs to a mud-stained Muse;
Let india-rubber pellets dance on grass
Where female arts the ruder sex surpass;
Let other people play at other things;
The king of games is still the game of kings.'

(JAMES KENNETH STEPHEN, *1891 and wondrous stuff it is.*)

This is clearly the early work of monks. It's played in a strange crypt-like gallery, full of irregularities. I played once at Petworth House with my uncle. It is a game designed for the more senior citizen, for young and keen though I was to get at the ball with the discarded snow-shoe that was provided as a bat, a right twit I was made to look in no time at all. (The bat is a fine status symbol to have lying in the back of your car. The odd aficionado will point and preen.) Uncle as I remember was up the end with the goal behind, a window full of netting. The floor was a maze of white lines and symbols ('hazard chase the door' is the cry if you land on one, and 'chase a yard worse than last gallery' another). His service, I could see that he had cut with some vigour, lobbed on to the roof of a shed that ran the length of the court to my right. I stood, mouth agape, as it bobbled and bounced along the roof, finally falling off and landing as dead as a taxidermist's dodo at my feet. I waved the snow-shoe at it vaguely, but there was no life left in it. It hadn't fallen far either.

It is a game of intense subtlety and with amazingly complicated rules. As I recall, one

There are only two clubs in the country, Queens in West Kensington and the Manchester Tennis and Racquet Club. If on the other hand you live near any of the following Public Schools: Charterhouse, Cheltenham, Clifton, Eton, Haileybury, Harrow, Malvern, Marlborough, Radley, Rugby, Tonbridge, Wellington or Winchester, get in touch with the master-in-charge. Wearing an old school tie of one of the other public schools (easily obtainable at many men's outfitters) might gain you easier entrée. All, except Cheltenham, have a resident professional, as do the two clubs, and I imagine that they, like the courts, lie fallow for much of the year. They are keen to make it more popular.

It's faster and hairier than squash, rackets do tend to crack and break under the strain as the ball is hit much harder, and they cost about £7. They confess it's a 'bit of a snob game in a way'. When they get too old for racquets they move on to real tennis, which is chess with violence.

Tennis and Racquets Association, 'Fairwater', Orchard Gate, Esher, Surrey.

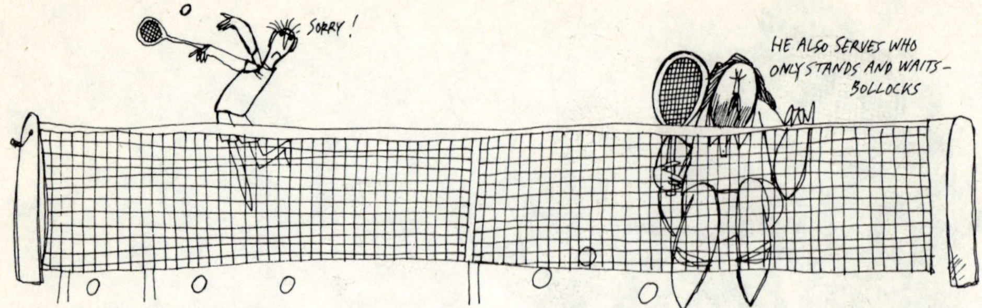

of the prime targets was a priest's hole some 40 feet above my head. I, in my turn, never got a single ball across the net. When I did, my uncle cleverly didn't bother to return it at all, thus gaining another point. I must sit down with the Rules for 10 years or so and brush up for my sporting dotage. Pierre Etchebaster was world champion until he was 60. That still only gives me 20 years.

There are 17 courts in the country – among the others are Queens, Lords Cricket Ground has one and there's Henry VIII's old patch at Hampton Court.

Note:
For those at either Oxford or Cambridge it is quite the simplest game at which to gain a 'blue'. It's only half a blue admittedly but they all count at I.C.I.

UNREAL TENNIS

Once again its antecedents are lost in the fogs of time, but one imagines that Henry VIII was lobbing away onto the shed roof and one of his wives said 'Henry, dear, couldn't you play outside, it's Madge's half-day and you know what she is?', and so he strode outside and, in a pet invented tennis as we know it. No sheds, no hazards, no priest's hole, I imagine he thought it half the game its father was. They called it tennis because it was viewed as polite to shout *'Tenez'* before serving, it would have been more British to have shouted 'Thar she blows!' or the like but a bloody silly name for a game at best. 'Over now to Wimbledon for the thar she blows and Dan Maskell.'

In the sort of tennis I played it was always seen as a disadvantage to have the serve. This doesn't seem to be the case at Wimbledon. I am constantly amazed at the incompetence of the receiver. It's the server who has his back to the railings where I come from. But then when I reveal that I usually play in wellingtons, you may have some small idea as to where that is. Definitely the public courts, hard by name but crumbling by nature. It's not a game I can ever remember playing wholly sober. There again, I see the distance from where I sit to Wimbledon, where sobriety seems all.

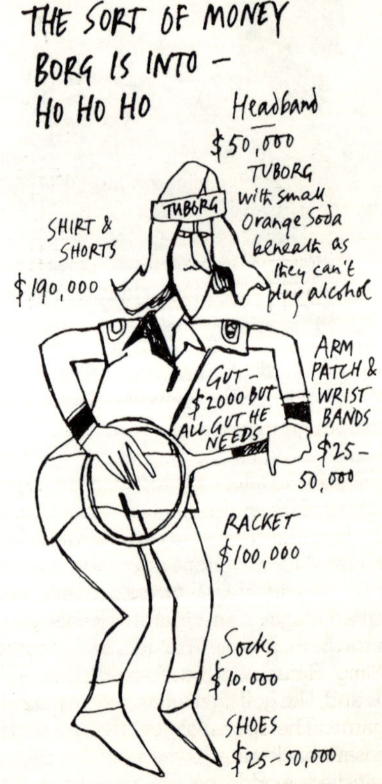

It's a fine spectator sport, particularly on television, though I've never fully understood why doubles is somehow less popular than singles. (The finest spectators are the Italians who boo and cheer, hiss and kiss each other and are much frowned upon at Wimbledon, bless them.) Doubles matches are far more incident-packed, and incidentally more enjoyable to play than singles. There are more of you to fetch the balls. Tennis, like golf, has become a travelling circus, with ludicrous financial rewards and, like golf again, has become another ball-game. The sports pages used to provide a pleasant back-water away from the priggish self-satisfied worlds of the boardroom and the Unions, the publicity men and the money-grabbers and grubbers. Now they reflect all the beastliness of the front page. Only the trousers are shorter.

An example of this. I was watching the Wightman Cup on the telly, and could barely believe my ears when I heard the commentator, it may have been Dan Maskell – it was a long, white-flannelled voice – saying, 'The American had a pain-killing injection before the game and if the English girl can prolong this set, the ankle may well give out'. I sat there thinking, has it come to this? This is the sort of daft, rhetorical question you often put to yourself when you feel that the limits of folly have been reached and some fool bounds over them in one, establishing a new world

TO TEST YOUR WITS

Two unique photographs, both taken from the rear. We have juggled with the captions, thus providing something of a brain-teaser.

A UNIQUE PHOTOGRAPH OF KING EDWARD

A remarkable interest attaches to the above photograph from the fact that it was taken by a loyal assistant who unawares "snapped" our late beloved King as he was posing for his photograph in the studio of a well-known Homburg photographer. Accustomed as we are to every kind of photograph of him in every imaginable attitude, the above little picture, so unusual and so characteristically posed, will perhaps recall his Majesty to many of us who on the racecourse, abroad, and elsewhere have seen him standing in this attitude, which is one he constantly fell into

Virginia Wade

◆バージニア・ウエード

〈**国籍**〉Great Britain イギリス。〈**生年月日**〉1945・7・10。〈**出身地**〉ボーンマス。〈**身長・体重**〉170.2cm，63kg。〈**戦歴**〉**1965～74** ワイトマン杯出場(12勝16敗)。**1966** 全米単ベスト8。ウィンブルドン複ベスト4(ジョーンズ)。米国内複ベスト4(ショー)。**1967** イタリアベスト8。ウィンブルドン単ベスト8，複ベスト4(ジョーンズ)。ロスマンズ英HC優勝(68/'73/'74)。英HC複優勝(ヘルドマン)，混合複優勝。フェデレーション杯出場(～74)。**1968** ウィンブルドンプレート優勝。全米優勝。南ア準優勝。イタリア複(コート)，英HC混合複(ハウ)優勝。**1969** 全米ベスト4。ディウォー杯優勝。国内ランキング1位。**1970** イタリアベスト4。全仏ベスト8。全米ベスト4。ロスマンズ英HC準優勝。南アベスト4。ウィンブルドン複準優勝(デュール)。**1971** イタリア優勝。南ア単ベスト4。グリーンシールドウェルシュ優勝。**1972** 全豪優勝。ウィンブルドン，全仏，全米単ベスト8，複準優勝(コート)。南ア，カナダ，アルゼンチン単準優勝。ディウォー杯，グリーンシールドウェルシュ準優勝。NSW準優勝。南ア混合複優勝(マリガン)。国内ランキング1位。**1973** 全豪，ウィンブルドン，全米ベスト8。南アベスト4。ディウォー杯優勝。NSWベスト4。全豪(コート)，全仏(コート)，全米(コート)，イタリア(モロゾワ)複優勝。南ア複準優勝(エバート)。国内ランキング1位。MBE(ブリティッシュエンパイア5等勲士)受賞。**1974** イタリアベスト8。ウィンブルドンベスト4。ディウォー杯優勝。全米複ベスト4(ハント)。英HC複優勝(ヘルドマン)。VSシカゴ，フェニックス優勝。モーリン・コノリー杯準優勝。WTT出場(ニューヨーク・セ

record. It has come to this, it has passed this, and it's gone further since I last mentioned it to you. Would we have made such a noise about Waterloo if we'd outnumbered the Frog 20-1 and their entire army had been suffering from terminal hernias? As it was, the ankle did give out and the English girl still lost, which was either old-fashioned British sportsmanship, misplaced many would say, or sold-fashioned British incompetence which seems more likely. Old-fashioned British sportsmanship, which sprang originally from our own feelings of superiority, and meant that we would patronisingly help the victim of our straight-left to his feet before the count only then to unleash a thumping upper-cut, (this was taken to laughable extremes on occasion, as when British officers would insist on the Thin Red Line firing second, what remained of it), has given way to new-fashioned British sportsmanship. This is to canvass widely every reason why you have no

There shall be galleries, hazards, penthouses and tambours
Thou shalt lay chases, the second bounce of thine ball
determining the chase thou hast laid. Ye chases shall be
measured from ye back wall. 'Better than half a yard shall be
best. Thou shalt crouch in ye commode position.
'Dead Nick' – the goodliest serve
Chases be white lines parallel to
ye net. We shall make up ye
Rules as we go along.
(Tune: Greensleeves)

chance of winning it against superior odds, or equally valid reasons for losing against inferior odds such as over-confidence, the advantages of the opposition of being under-dog, thin skin over the eyebrows or the lack of meat after the War again.

Meanwhile, back on Court 1. Unless you're extremely fortunate public courts have certain hazards. The most obvious will be found underfoot, there are also the wild bunch playing either side of you, serving and lobbing into your court and nicking your balls, and also the fact that you can usually only hire a court for an hour.

The mention of tennis clubs can send Martin Chivers running up and down your spine. You instantly picture scenes from Noel Coward's *Peyton Place* or Barbara Cartland's *Naked Lunch*. Research has proved that you're probably right. Somewhere there is a tennis club for you. Be wary. You can't go far wrong with the tennis side of it, which you may well think is the most important, once more you err. To err is human, to um and er and then find yourself in charge of teas, suppers, the barbecue, decorating the disco, changing the records, dancing with the Hon. President's wife is sheer bloody lunacy.

On the playing side you're covered. Most clubs ask you to 'play yourself in', so that they can see if you're up to standard or down to it. This works both ways and means you're in there with fellow-members as good, bad or average as you are. If it's tennis you're after.

It's the social side you have to watch closely, but not knowing you socially I can't really help you. You may long have wished to star in Coward's *Peyton Place*, I once walked on in it as second wife-swapper, but unfortunately threw my car keys too far down-stage and eight female members of the cast fell into the orchestra pit scrambling for them. It wasn't a good evening, there was an R.S.P.C.A. raid during the famous Cat-Gutting Chorus.

BADMINTON

Badminton comes out of Battledore by Shuttlecock, but the Army in India, sticklers for the proprieties even at 110 degrees in the shade and sensible of there being ladies present, called it Poona rather than Battlecock. In 1870 a gang of them weekended at the Duke of Beaufort's, introduced Poona to the assembly and as some sort of tribute to the Duke renamed the game badminton, after his seat. Another pity, really.

The joy of the game is you can play it indoors or outdoors and don't need a great deal of room, the official dimensions of the court are 20 foot by 40 foot, but you can always make local rules. I've played it in the Dordogne

in thick nettles, but then I've lived. A disadvantage of outdoor play is that the antic wind can play merry hell with your shuttlecock. Sports centres will provide all the indoor facilities, and you can study the sport at evening classes. If however you want to play in tournaments, get in among the Malays, who seem the chief stumbling-block on the way to the top, join a club. The kit is all white and basic, and subs around £10 a year.

There is something deeply satisfying about hitting a shuttlecock cleanly with a racket. Admittedly, all we had in the nettles were cheap Hong Kong plastic ones which disintegrated almost immediately with the plastic feathers fluttering past your ear like autumn leaves. Even then the 'poink' it made was deeply satisfying. It rates, to my mind, with leather on willow and smoked mackerel smacked against a bare belly.

Badminton Association of England, 44/45 Palace Road, Bromley, Kent.

Scottish Badminton Union, 8 Frederick Street, Edinburgh.

Welsh Badminton Union, 7 Romsley Court, St Dials, Cwmbran.

Badminton Union of Ireland, Derryveagh, Saval Park Road, Dalkey, Co. Dublin.

JAI ALAI OR PELOTA

I can't really recommend that you take this up, as you'll very rarely get a game over here, even if you find a court, which you won't, but as a spectator sport it stands supreme. Madmen, usually of Spanish origin, with lengthy baskets tied to their wrists send a hard goatskin ball sometimes a good 50 yards and at a speed of at least 200 m.p.h. in a long, thin three-sided court. I've only seen it once when I was in Mexico City. The excitement at 7000 feet was almost my undoing.

The pleasure for the spectator is the incessant gambling. I being less courageous, placed my bets at the Tote before the game, and then missed most of the game as I was watching the harder gamblers at work throughout the run of play. What happens is that between the stands and the court the bookies parade, neatly clad and instantly recognisable in red berets and blazers. They are equipped with tennis balls, ready slit to take money and betting-slips. At a signal from the back of the stand, the bookie throws the ball with great accuracy to the punter, who pops money and bet in the ball, and returns it with equal bravura. There was one old gentleman juggling constantly with three bookmakers at a time.

A rare and mystic sporting experience. There was cock-fighting down the road, but I drew the line at that.

Next day, however, I went to a gloriously tatty Pro/Am bull-fight some distance from Mexico City, and whereas I was delighted at the half-time score – Bulls 8, Matadors 0, the crowd was whistling furiously and throwing cushions. The band left in a huff, so that the music that drove Ernest Hemingway to distraction, had to be played over the tannoy on a gramophone. I think the result finally was a draw, I remember a pro, clearly mid-field sweeper for Mexico City, being brought on and he would stand no nonsense from any bull, hence possibly the term 'taking no bull' coined on the horns of an enema.

However, if asked to hand out prizes for bravery in the face of sport, I shall ignore Japanese gymnasts with broken legs, or short-sighted racing-drivers, or punch-drunk croquet champions, and plump for a tiny Mexican amateur matador who was gored in the upper thigh in the first minute, to return bandage over trouser 10 minutes later to vast acclaim only to be briskly holed in the other leg. As he was dragged off waving by the stadium tractor, the crowd cheered, the band wept, and I realised that, in the land of the legless, hop-scotch is impossible.

You could become the first British bull-fighter, but it's been done already by El Higgins, and you can hardly follow that.

Cost of joining club – *exorbitant.*
Insurance – *high.*
Price of costume – *ludicrous, unless you knit your own.*

POTTING AND PUTTING

SNOOKER

Since colour television revealed to a startled world that the sky was blue, Rod Laver's hair was orange, snooker balls were not in varying shades of grey and the cloth was in a quite different shade of green from the players' dinner-jackets, interest in the sport has burgeoned. Not that it wasn't always popular and rightly, but now spectators are packing out tournaments. You can fill a theatre easily with a good cast. The performers appear to be the most delightful of sportsmen, but then only good can come from any man with a misspent youth and the sartorial elan of Al Capone's Chicago Allstars.

I was lucky to spend the War years with my Welsh grandfather, a G.P. in Newport, Monmouthshire, whose sole relaxation apart from Vera Lynn, to whom his ear was clapped at every opportunity, was snooker. I spent happy hours watching him circle the table, whistling tunelessly. So I was armed with the rudiments at an early age. Unfortunately I didn't meet a table again for 10 years and that was in a NAAFI club in Germany. As some sort of fitness and physical efficiency was called for by the militia, I put myself down for beer and snooker. They drew the line at enormous, vast-breasted Valkyri, alas, and I was instead forced to carry a fellow-squaddie in full battle-order for 100 yards to prove my powers of strength and endurance met with the Army's approval. It would, I suppose, be contrary to the Official Secrets Act to reveal that the only weapon I'd ever been issued with was a typewriter. Perhaps I was expected to counter the thrust of the oncoming Russian hordes by laying about me with said fellow-squaddie. Suffice to say I picked the smallest I could find, a tiny Scots cook corporal, wizened with age, a man whose *Bombe Surprise* had baffled more than one disposal squad, and parking the elfin chef on my shoulder, trotted the 100 yards in no time at all. A new record. Picture if you will the look of anguish in the old poison dwarf's rheumy eye when the sergeant-major barked 'Change partners!' I then weighed a good 16 stone, my packs were full of books, and my little friend was close to retirement. However, we created a rude beast with four legs and embarked on the long journey together, he bent with stress and strain, and I gasping on tiptoe, indelibly scarring my polished boots as we went. So much for physical fatness.

There was another long gap until I played again. My wife was fortunately keen on the game and we finally found a home with a room large enough to house a three-quarter size table, which I found in the *Exchange and Mart.* Reconditioned, legs of your choice, balls, cues and a score-board for £80 odd.

It was worth giving up the bedroom for this source of constant joy. It's now given way to an even greater sense of constant joy – one small son, but I have this sneaking suspicion that

no home is truly complete without one. Sleep on it, you cry, and I thank you. You may have hit on the very solution.

Constant practice is the keynote to success. I can't imagine that any other sport requires more. There must be a billiards table near you somewhere, perhaps one of those great halls, dark green and friendly, with the relaxing click of drawling cicadas. That's where you'll learn the most, the older members will see you right. You can attend evening classes on the subject, and sports centres provide most of the necessary facilities, but none of the necessary atmosphere.

There are 70,000 clubs in Britain, your local library will give you the address of your local association, or write to *The Billiards and Snooker Foundation, 145 Oxford Street, London W1R 1TB*, or again *The World Billiard and Snooker Control Council* (which sounds ominously like a branch of the Festival of Light), *Alexandra Chambers, 32 John William Street, Huddersfield, West Yorkshire.* I met Joe Davis once ('Have you met Joe Davis?' some fool once asked him: 'I've slept with his wife', he replied cheerfully), some time after he retired. Apparently he has never picked up a cue since. There is a lesson there somewhere.

BILLIARDS

Although snooker is the favourite, don't forget the pleasures of billiards, an even more subtle and accomplished game with far fewer balls, the cannon and the in-off. The only drawback in clubs, pubs, etc. is that the lights rarely stay on long enough for a good game, but you can invariably finish a frame in the time allotted.

Pool

Pool is worth a look as well. As the table's smaller, quite a few pubs seem to be installing it. The pockets seem larger too, which can be a comfort.

GOLF

(*Pronounced goff, goalf, golf or goaf depending on how silly you are.*)

It's an addiction, and like most addictions extremely expensive, hard to kick, and it renders you fearsomely boring to all those not hooked to whatever turns you on. Golfers become extremely irritable and edgy when they can't get a fix, and when fixed, vanish into a world of their own in which for three hours or so they believe they are Johnny Miller or Lee Trevino. The withdrawal symptoms are beastly to observe, usually incoherent babbling about missed birdies and eagles that never dared. Never be waylaid in conversation by a golfer, particularly if he's recently shot an albatross.

I confess that I was once hooked, doctor, and played regularly for about two years, and a bad-tempered, petulant, insufferable bore I became, reliving every hole as if it was an old war-wound. National Service, bless it, cured me, and I've only played three times in the last 15 years, in California, Ireland and Australia – there's jet-lag for you. What a wonder-

ful game it is when you don't give a stuff. You're relaxed, your swing is variable but free, you laugh at air-shots, roll roaring in the sand-traps, and all you remember as you sink ale later is the one good shot among the 130 played. The less often you play, the more exercise you get, and the more exciting and unexpected the views of the course. It becomes simply a pleasant walk in the country, hitting a golf ball occasionally instead of lopping the tops off thistles with your sword-stick. I can't fathom the minds of those who wish to go round in 69, I like to hit the ball a few more times than that, and fairways are intensely dull to travel on. Like autobahns.

It's an ancient game emanating as you know from Scotland. (D-----d Scotch croquet, as I have seen it referred to.) A sobering thought, *en passant*, is that several golf club secretaries were killed at Culloden. This has not prevented many of them from soldiering on in office. Its popularity I would like to think stems from man's constant urge to battle against nature and the elements, pitting himself against the rugged grandeur of the seventeenth at St Mac-Something's, or carving a bogey through the shifting, whispering sand-hills of Lytham St Someone Else. I think I found a little of myself once searching out my ball among a clump of gum trees, the kookaburras laughing gleefully in their branches koalas snorting, God in his heaven and another hole in 27.

Alas, I doubt it, golfers are about as romantic as astronauts or racing cyclists. They see a ball, they see a flag, they pick a club, they thrash a caddie. Nature they scorn. There's a lively argument afoot at the moment that golf is going soft, that the essential character of the game, the traditional values, the afore-mentioned mud-wrestling with Mother Nature, are becoming things of the past. The essence of golf is that just as you're cruising along in par, seething with confidence and putting like a dream, God in his wisdom, suddenly and violently strikes you down with a sand storm, a

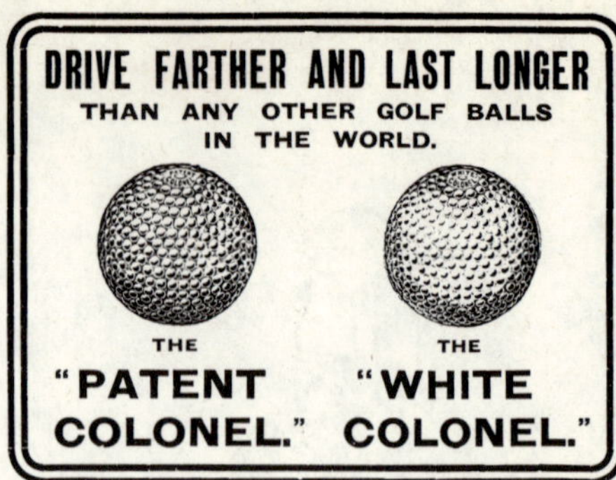

fit of slicing or a plague of casual water. The true golfer is he who can rise above the slings and arrows, the sharp switches in his outrageous fortunes, can take the rough as well as the fairway, the bad lie with the good.

The hard men point to the death of the stymie in 1951. They suggest that rules allowing teeing-up on fairways, wiping mud off your ball prior to putting, the repair of dents where a previous shot has pitched, and free drops if you chance upon a pathway or the like, are all emasculating the game and removing the necessary pressures on the brain and spirit that made golfers what they were and aren't any longer. They are much more cosseted today and not only those at the top where the pressures that still exist are largely financial. It isn't after all only the golfer who suffers when he misses the Open Championship by six inches on the eighteenth green, but very possibly his chain of woolly cap emporia, his range of autographed niblicks, his personalised golf bags and mechanised caddies. If we lose the occasional spectacle of a famed pro chipping back-handed out of a natural hazard like a rhododendron bush, then we lose a large lump of what golf is all about. Blisters and brain damage.

I tend to agree with this view. It is being ironed out and prettied up for the small screen, and whereas we at home rejoice in the spectacle of Caspar from a muddy lie, shanking the ball between his legs, straight along the ground for 20 yards, this is not what they would like to see. We're into hyper-heroes now and whereas we can fork out money to look like them, (and the costume becomes more garish and absurd by the round) spend a fortune on similar clubs and bags and the other jew-jaws on display, we are also forced to adopt their single-mindedness and brow-ploughing intensity.

I might be forced back on the links if only to propagate once more the joys of bad, laughing golf. You would only be allowed eight clubs, none known only by numbers, but grand old clubs like spoons and mashies, niblicks and blasters, and wooden-shafted putters. No tartan caps with pom-poms, or short-brimmed canvas trilbies, or worst of all those S.S.-Surplus peaked affairs. Plus-fours would be compulsory, waistcoats optional and all 18 holes need not necessarily be played. A frown or muffled curse would cost a shot. It would be a pleasure.

The Stymie as was.

Some hoary old Jokes to enliven those balls-aching moments at the Nineteenth

As it is, apart from my irregular international golf, and I remember with pride going round the Royal Australian Golf Club's putting green in 34, my only recent outing was at the Savoy Hotel. For some reason best known to them and none the worse for that, American Express asked me to a party there to meet Jack Nicklaus. One of the side-shows was a putting contest over carpet, you were allowed three putts and anyone who holed out in the Jack Nicklaus Autographed Indoor Hole won a Jack Nicklaus Autographed Putter. Few succeeded, but finally full of Pimm's Number One, I volunteered. As I said, relaxation is the name of the game. It was a 15-yarder. My first putt, which for laughter value I essayed as an in-off off the bar, lay dead. My second, more traditional, lay deader. Laughing uproariously and with cries of 'Easy' I holed the third. It was worth it for the green eyes of the

A famous moment. The author receives his only golf club from the Master. Admit it, you always thought he was taller.

golf-bitten. The Great Bear himself presented me with the signed weapon. If you only have one golf club, I said to him, then this is the one to have. I couldn't say fairer. It stands now still wrapped in polythene in pride of place leaning nonchalantly against the telly. Perhaps it would be wiser to stop while I'm ahead. Re-reading the last paragraph it proves my point that all golf stories are at heart boring. I shall stop.

One favourable aspect of the game is that it transfers well to print, be it Henry Longhurst or P. G. Wodehouse. Apart from cricket, it does attract the best writers. Unlike football, which attracts the most pretentious. On the other hand it has the largest fund of awful jokes, many oddly starring God or his eldest.

Where to

There are public courses, open to all, and offering rare opportunities for bad golf. If you want competition, however, and a handicap you must join a golf club. There are 2000-odd listed in *Golfers' Handbook.* You'll need a proposer and a seconder, evidence at most of previous experience or tuition (£1.50-£5 for half an hour from a club pro) and you'll probably end up on a waiting list. You could simply pay the occasional green fee, which comes cheaper on a week-day, but not that cheap. Membership fees vary. £20-£250 for joining, and anything from £50 to £100 and upwards per annum, or through the nostril if you prefer.

The equipment is far from cheap, but you could get a second-hand bag of clubs for £50 or so.

You can always go to a golf range and get down to the nitty-gritty of golf, which is trying to hit the bloody thing at all. I shall stick to the putting course on Folkestone's Leas, and try and hole the Tower of London in one with my Jack Nicklaus White Fang.

This chapter concerns Team Ball Games. Let the picture below of Billingsworth Tidy Amateur Rugby League team seen here after losing the Grand Final of the 1976 Cup serve as a terrible warning to you.

BASEBALL

And why not, you chauvinistic swine? Believing the game to be stone cold dead in the market, although old memories would be rekindled by the Baseball Ground, where Derby County play football, we found this not to be the case at all. There is a *British Amateur Baseball Federation* at *197 Newbridge Road, Hull, North Humberside*, and from them we learnt that there are some 45 clubs in Britain. They tend to gravitate around American Service bases, the four main areas being Merseyside, Humberside, the Midlands and there's a Southern League. The London teams are stiff with Americans, but this is hardly surprising, they are avenging the introduction of cricket to Hollywood in the 1920s by C. Aubrey Smith. And at the same time enjoying our falling pound. They'll all be gone, I expect, when the oil starts pouring in. So will we.

It started when Englishmen in America (few naturally embarked without their cricket-bags) found themselves so occupied with winning the West, seeing off Apaches, building a New World, there was never any time for a decent five-day cricket match, nor a decent pitch from the Atlantic to the Pacific. So they invented baseball. To start with you threw a cricket ball at the runner, but this proving unnecessarily painful, they came up with bases. These were stumps on which many a runner became impaled, so flat stones or 'plates' were introduced. In 1845 the cricketers started the Knickerbocker Baseball Club of New York, and drew up fresh rules. They reasoned for instance that a diamond was easier to run around than a square. In their first game alas the Knickerbockers were wiped out by The New York Nine, and went back to cricket. The winners played on. The game finally took off when the Cincinnati Red Stockings turned professional in the 1870s.

I only mention all this to make cricketers feel better and to give the lie to the 'rounders' slur.

Also our baseball gentleman said that the difficulty in getting the game accepted here was that people identify it with the Harlem Globetrotters (a wonderful sequence of non-sequiturs) or know nothing of it at all save for distant memories of a film about Babe Ruth with Gary Cooper in it. (Cineasts may remember *The Pride of the Yankees* – 1942, I don't, but I've just looked it up.) Come along then, let boldness be your friend.

One of the clubs will instruct you (one such the Kensington Spirit of '76 – a charming name), and probably kit you out. The uniforms are extremely smart, but expensive. One of those gloves with a hole in it, can cost anything from £4 to £30. What an interesting Christmas gift though.

The point is, according to our source, that

given the slightest aptitude for ball games, you could play for Britain in next to no time. Our international team is apparently not very good.

If you think baseball is not for you, at a twilight League match at Roehampton not so long ago, an English international was sent off, and then had a fine punch-up with the umpire. In the clubroom later, bottles flew, the umpire was laid out, one of the promoters concussed and another struck in the face by a sandwich. There, I told you, it might well be the game for you, dear. How nice to play America away.

BASKETBALL AND NETBALL

It's associated here with netball, a girlish pursuit but popular, some 2000 clubs play that. Funnily enough, in America you can be a national basketball hero, where the game is enormous and, apart from the Harlem Globetrotters, taken extremely seriously. Height is the great thing. You may remember at Montreal the huge seven-foot woman, Rumanian I think, who staggered about like King Kong but who, if the ball was pressed into her ham-like hands, could drop the ball into the basket with deadly effect. One opposing lady succeeded in dribbling ball and herself through Kong's legs. Incidentally, I have a brilliant notion for a sequel to King Kong, set at the poor creature's funeral. It could be a classic disaster film as the cremation gets out of hand and sets fire to most of the West Coast of America.

There are 1000 clubs all eager for your attentions if you are a male over six foot five inches or a five foot eleven inch female. My word, I only just fail to qualify as a woman.

The kit is minimal, but baggy on most of us. If you are extremely tall then, the Great Britain Netball side needs you, but hurry, they are apparently fast improving.

Addresses from *All England Netball Association, 70 Brompton Road, London SW3*. Or *English Basketball Association, Calomax House, Lupton Avenue, Leeds 9*. Take your pick, long-arse!

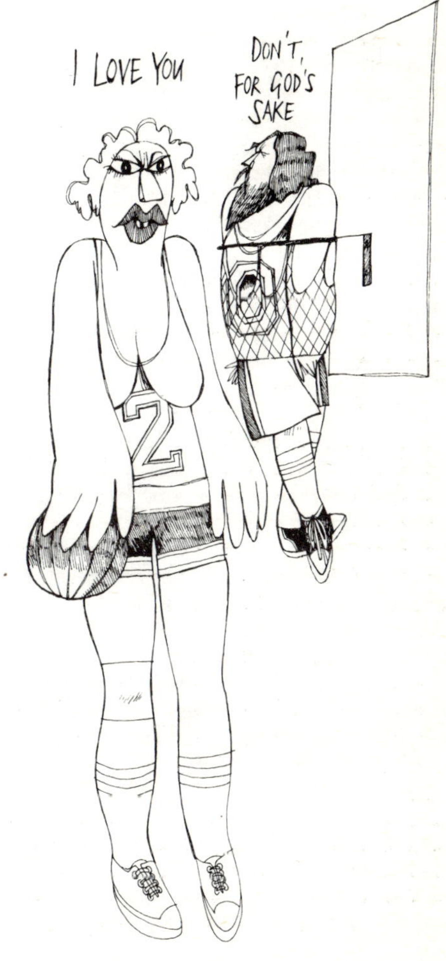

HOCKEY

It's a funny thing but when the twin domes appear as they sometimes do on sporting programmes, I heave the smallest of sighs, put on a record of vocal refrain singing *Autumn Leaves*, and think nostalgically that once I dallied with an English centre-forward who scored at Wembley. A lady hockey player I hasten to add (before Malcolm Macdonald becomes the object of strange looks in the communal bath), but she had remarkably well-preserved shins.

There is mixed hockey apparently, though perhaps if I'd known that at the time I might not be alive today. I must say one of the sporting rôles I would be least eager to fill is that of a hockey goalkeeper. There can be few more fearsome jobs on earth. The ball is extremely hard and the hockey stick is a famed offensive weapon. Ronald Searle armed the girls of St Trinian's with them, and I think 'Bulldog' Drummond used them when he and his mates pulled socks over their heads and went off to beat up Jews. Perhaps it was tennis rackets. Either way he is one of the least attractive figures in fiction.

The kit is basic, a stick should be easy to come by, shin-pads or paperback books stuffed down the front of socks are highly recommended. Unless you played at school I'd forget it. 'Bully off!' you cry. Very well.

Lists of the women's clubs from the *All England Women's Hockey Association, 160 Great Portland Street, London W1N 5TB.*

Men's clubs from *The Hockey Association, 70 Brompton Road, London SW3 1EX.*

ICE HOCKEY

I'm fairly certain that back in the dim and distant we had our own ice hockey heroes in *Champion* or *Hotspur* or possibly *Wizard*, but something about the sport clearly didn't set the British crowd alight, and by the end of the 1950s professional ice hockey was as dead and deeply buried as a hairy mammoth in aspic. The London Lions hung on till the early 1970s but to little avail. They've tried to popularise it on the television but it's so brisk and far away that you can't actually see a puck. Still, it excites Canadians, and that in itself is no mean feat. It has a vivid and colourful catalogue of foul plays, you can be up before the Beak for charging, spearing, butting, ending, tripping and slashing. Throwing the

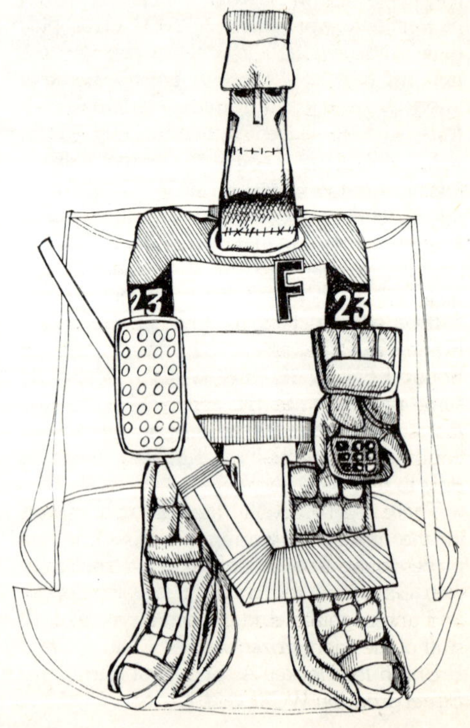

stick or handling the puck are not encouraged and clipping, hooking, holding or kicking can all end in that most brilliant of sporting innovations, the penalty bench, 'ice box' or 'cooler'. Would that it featured in other sports. A public display of guilt, not unlike the stocks, would prove far more of a deterrent than even the prospect of an early bath with Eddie Waring.

The hairy mammoth is apparently thawing out, but not without considerable difficulty. It is generally accepted that it's best to start the game when young. American, Canadian and Central European teams all average about 20 years of age or younger. Picture then the sorry spectacle of our future prospects, keen young 15-year-olds taking to what little ice we have to offer at one o'clock in the night. Even then gangs of speed-skaters or dancing pairs are pacing up and down impatiently waiting for use of the ice. Some have travelled 100 miles to find some. Apart from the obvious feeling that God is not entirely on your side, not to mention the Powers That Be, the equipment is not cheap and impossible to hire – the helmets, the padding, the skates, the stick.

It's a sad fact that, for instance, the Silver Blades in Streatham is the only ice-rink in South London, an area which enjoys the same population as Switzerland. Further sad fact – ice hockey is more popular in this country than ever before, but clearly available only to teenage insomniacs.

There are 14 clubs in the south and seven in the north, all with coaches, some ex-professionals from the old days of the Wembley Lions and the Brighton Tigers, unpaid and unrecognised, and desperate for the very stuff of the sport, frozen water.

British Ice Hockey Association, 20 Bedford Street, London WC2E 9HP.

CURLING

There's little chance of this in England, the ice being packed 24 hours a day with all manners of activity, but in Scotland skaters are only allowed on the ice at weekends and even then the curlers, whose natural home it is, whine like bog-pipes. Curling is a good money-spinner and they can afford to keep the skaters at bay.

It's a social game – and as you may know to your cost social in Scotland spells 'usquebaugh' – the water of life. Indeed this is the major expense. A session of curling costs about £1, but the *après*-curling can get pleasantly out of hand. Time is also consumed, particularly if you get involved in a club or league, but a good reason for taking it up however is that you need not be in the least young or athletic, although the stone weighs 40 pounds, you only have to move it to and fro, you don't have to lift it. To avoid taking off with it towards the distant 'brush' your foot is on a launching-pad attached to the ice, called a crampit or hack. The only energetic bit is the sweeping which keeps your stone moving faster or longer, and as it slows down it 'takes the handle' or reacts to the bias you put on it yards back. The object of the game is virtually the same as bowls, played in the main between teams or rinks of four. (There are pairs competitions.)

Gordon Richards was, and possibly still is, an aficionado. The Royal Caledonian Curling Club is in Edinburgh, as it should be. Should Glasgow feel left out, take heart Glaswegians from your tourist leaflet enticingly named *Ihr Ferienzel in Schöttland.* Maurice Chevalier, it says, *war gezuhrt und begeistert. 'Mon Dieu', sagte er, 'Kein wunder* Harry Lauder *liebte diest Stadt so sehr'.* Don't you feel better now?

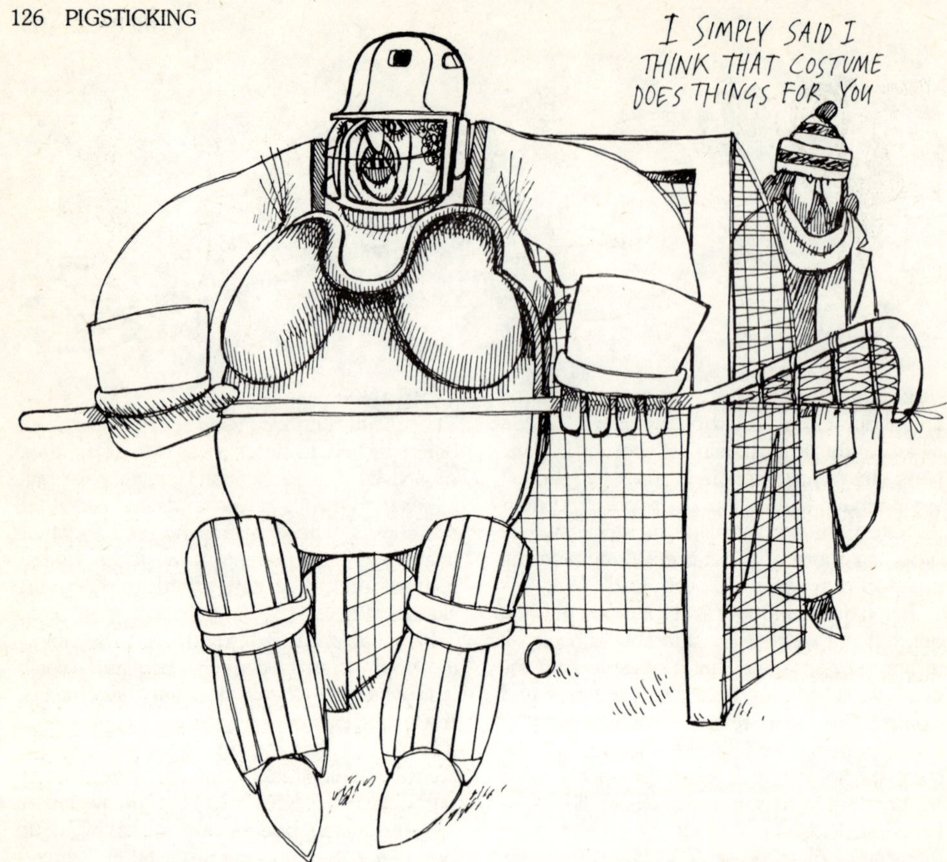

LACROSSE
The sport of my mad mother. Poor thing, she has scar tissue over each eye like Henry Cooper as a result of early lacrosse. Not *early* lacrosse as in Baggataway, the popular inter-tribal version of the game as played between the Comanches and the Sioux. Many the tribal conflict that arose from early lacrosse hooliganism. Mother has never to my knowledge mingled in Red Indian circles, though the Welsh did, of course, discover America. Even so I meant lacrosse early in her life.

If hockey takes it on your shins, lacrosse a more aerial sport, takes it out on your brains or between the eyes. It's a very fast game, the ball leaves the netted stick or 'crosse', not unlike a primitive device for catching large moths, at tremendous pace and trapping it in your own net requires a high degree of skill. You also need to be supremely fit as the pitch is 110 yards by 60 yards, some have no boundaries at all, either way there is a good deal of ground to be covered.

The gentlemen start with a 'face', while the ladies begin with a 'draw'. I'm sure there is a very good reason for this. While the gentlemen play four 'quarters' of 15 minutes each, the ladies are satisfied with 25 minutes each way. As the game hasn't gone professional I imagine there will be no demands for equal pay for less work as in tennis.

Gentlemen should apply for information to the *Hon. Secretary (R. Balls), English Lacrosse Union, 64 Broadway, Hockley, Essex*; ladies to the *All England Women's Lacrosse Association, 70 Brompton Road, London SW3 1EX*.

KORFBALL
I've mentioned briefly the origins of Eton Fives and the fact that it evolved from a simple ball game played amongst some of the architectural extravagances at the back of Eton College Chapel by Etonians, not monks as illustrated, but I prefer drawing monks to drawing Etonians (if poets can have licence

why can't I?). The reason I mention it again is that the sports that slowly matured over the centuries are to my mind so infinitely superior to those clearly invented by committees to fit modern gymnasia or aircraft hangars, which would be the more interesting if they left the planes where they were. That is why I have little time for basketball or netball or handball, the latter I refuse to mention at all, being an elephantine exercise, clearly thought up by the interior decorators of the Tower of Babel.

I think I enjoyed Eton Fives more than any other game I've ever played. This is despite the fact that I was once humiliated by the Eton First Pair in the Public Schools Fives Competition. They turned up an hour late in a Rolls Royce, supercilious and far from apologetic. Wracked with bubbling bile and apprehension, my first stroke was an air-shot of such violence that I stunned myself momentarily on the buttress, and they won Game-1, Game-1, Game-5. How they laughed, the glib swine. I realised then that even within the Public School system there were gross inequalities. Still, it was something to see my name two days running in the sports pages of *The Times*, even as W. Lushton. The reason I haven't otherwise recommended this princely game is that it's almost impossible to get one in the after-life. It's strictly Public School only and I have a nasty suspicion that come the Revolution, rather than throwing the game open to all, they'll use the courts to store ammunition.

Howeverbeitmoresothere, there is one game invented in this country and played in Britain and others parts of the globe that seems to have its attractions.

A Dutch schoolmaster was undergoing a refresher course in woodwork in a small Swedish village at the turn of the century, and came upon a game not entirely unlike basketball, but he liked it and he took the idea back with him to Amsterdam. His school was coeducational, and he was having trouble exercising his girls, so he drew up the rules of this new game which involved teams of six of one sex and half a dozen of the other. He christened it korfball, as korf is Dutch for basket, and it is two of these bottomless costerlike baskets mounted on poles at either end of the pitch that form the object of the game. Alright, it's not the most original idea in the

world, but the mixed bit is quite jolly and the sport hath charms. The pitch is divided into three and you have two men and two women in each section. There's an indoor version, micro korfball, with only two sections and eight players per team. This can also be played outside when space is limited. Attack, defence and midfield. One advantage is that there are no positions, as the players change sections after every two goals. There is not only equality of sexes but also of opportunity. Utopia looms. Perhaps you didn't know they played korfball in Utopia.

The rules are simple. There's no running with the ball, no kicking, no hitting, no tackling or holding, no violence, it's all swift passing and team-work and observation of the old niceties, sportsmanship as was and the giving of flowers to fellow-korfers. Not only are we advised that many marriages spring from the game (the reverse is the case in most other sports), but this could represent one of your best chances of playing for Great Britain.

The game is played in south-east London and Maidstone in the main at the moment. There are 23 clubs or so, with a £3 subscription and a token 25p per game. The British Korfball Association get a lot of requests from abroad for exchange teams, and it is clear they are eager for participants.

The British Korfball Association, 35 Langley Oaks Avenue, Sanderstead, Surrey.

VOLLEYBALL

I have very little to say about this. I think the attractions of this stop at the lithe and lovely Japanese ladies, the opposition in most cases looked desperate at best. If you have a mild longing to be a famous volleyballer, then I suggest you seek employment in a Japanese factory, and worry over tiny, transistorised,

miniaturised differentials. I feel at heart that the game was designed for the beach, a large ball and a length of rope being all you need, but to see adults at it in hot and cold running blood at such as the Olympics is as silly as International Blindman's Buff or Olympic Pig-in-the-Middle.

Still, it keeps the Nipponese executives in trim and at the higher levels is extremely energetic. There are about 200 clubs affiliated to the *English Volleyball Association, 128 Melton Road, West Bridgford, Nottingham,* an annual membership fee being about £5.

'Spiking' is the only technical phrase. As the ball comes over the net, one player knocks it in the air, the second plays it high and close to the net and the third 'spikes' it or slams it down at the opposition's floor-space. That anything so banal should be named after that wise, good person borders on the criminally inane. *En passant,* dare I mention a life-long objection to the squeak of rubber boot on polished wooden floor, it raises the hackles like the noise of a razor across teeth.

Noise Abatement Society, 6 Old Bond Street, W.1.

A distinguished Team of Famous Bearded People, winners of the John Player Dot-Cricket Cup for 103 consecutive years! (Seated L to R) Claus, S., Marx, K., Milligan, S. (Capt.), Shaw, G. B., Toulouse-Lautrec, H. (Standing L to R) VII, Edward the., Grace, D. W. G., Christ, J., Castro, F., Rasputin. I.. Shakespeare, W.

CRICKET

Apart from chess, and cricket is not unlike chess with violence, it is also quite the best documented game. You can study score-cards and averages, there are detailed maps of Bradman's first innings pin-pointing the direction of every scoring stroke, Larwood's m.p.h. and you can go to the lavatory with a 1926 *Wisden* and not be seen for a year. The only figures I understand are cricket statistics. And again no game has been blessed with better writing and reporting. Of course, cricket encourages it, it is a deeply poetic exercise. Admittedly, there's time to spare for the commentator to pick the *bon mot*, to compose the better metaphor, bed out and mulch the flowerier phrase, but football commentators succeed in deflowering more phrases per *Match of the Day* than Attila the Hun at his most lyrical. Name one football writer or commentator that holds a candle to Neville Cardus, John Arlott or Jack Fingleton, to name but three. And the illustrations are lousy as well and they have no excuse as there's certainly no shortage of incident in football and a far wider range of colours. I suppose cricket's advantages on that score are that the weather is warmer, the day is longer, the pace of the game more conducive to peaceful reflection and good conversation, and the writers and artists who love it feel freer to dwell on its grace and beauty compared with the blood, guts and twisted ligaments that excite their footballing equivalents. Statham's run-up and delivery could be described in almost balletic terms with not a cry of 'Poofy beyond!', whereas Malcolm Macdonald belting upfield goalwards will at best be compared with a runaway meat-wagon on the M33.

To prove the pleasure gained by thumbing through cricket's back numbers, inspired by the Centennial Test Match in Melbourne in March 1977, I was poring over some dusty tome and discovered to my joy that March 1877 wasn't the date to be commemorating at all. In the summer of 1868 the first Australian side visited England, and first Australians they were in more senses than one being a team of

'Aborigines', said a knowing friend, 'are vegetables'. 'Not so', I replied, 'they are the indigenous folk of Australia. You are thinking of aubergines.' He glanced nervously at his watch. 'Jesus Christ!', he cried, 'I must telephone the wife immediately', and away he sped. His wife is a disciple of Fanny Cradock, and he is always prepared for the worst.

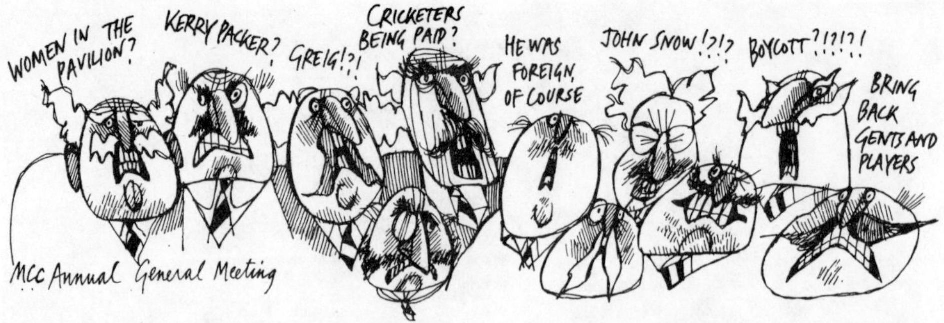

Aborigines, 13 in all, from the Werrumbrook tribe in Victoria. What a cheerful team they sound. Dick-a-Dick, Tiger, Mullagh and Bullocky, Sundown, Redcap, Twopenny and King Cole, Jim Crow and the unlikely Charlie Dumas. They played 47 matches in all, won 14, lost 14 and drew 19 and enormous crowds. Part of their crowd-pulling can be attributed to the displays they laid on at the end of a day's play. Dick-a-Dick for instance would stand in the middle of the pitch, armed with his war-shield and his 'nulla-nulla' and, with extraordinary agility and skill, fend off showers of cricket balls that the customers hurled at him. It cannot have been unlike facing the fury of a thousand Lillees. There was also, of course, advanced boomerang-throwing.

Incidentally, it occurred to me that given our gracious Queen's stoic behaviour in the face of Australian hostility and aggression, her regal warding-off of low flying placards and the like, she might well have been the answer to Dennis Lillee and should have been persuaded to pad up and make a game of it. In fact, England did make something of their second innings. How long ago that all seems now.

The Australians are a fine old enemy. I remember setting off to Australia for the first time during the M.C.C. tour there of 1964-65. Actually, I was in pursuit of my wife-to-be, not to mention wife-as-is. She, dear heart, having welcomed me with open arms to her native land in the small hours of the morning I arrived, then with a laudable sense of priorities, gave me a ticket to the England-Australia Test at Sydney Oval. All my Christmases at once. I sat in the pavilion in the boiling sun protected only by a small pork-pie hat, reddening and peeling by the minute but wrapped in a wonderful opening stand by Geoff Boycott and Bob Barber. Barber alone made 185, and they despatched the Australian bowlers to all corners of the ground. At the tea interval I was sitting quietly enjoying a beer or three, my first encounter with Resch's Dinner Ale and far from last, when an aged Australian with a face like a map of the Northern Territories, sat beside me and began to extol the virtues of Barber and Boycott. 'Jeeze', he said in his quaint Australian manner, 'them two is showing our bloody lot how to bat. Bloody beautiful. Bloody Booth could take a bloody lesson from bloody Barber.' 'Sir', I said, flushed with pride and a fourth Resch, 'how glad I am to hear all this, for I arrived only this morning from the Old Dart and – '. I saw the map of the Northern Territories twist and pale as if in the grips of Hurricane Marcia, he rose as a man and with a wild cry of 'Farking Pom!' vanished from my ken.

I've played cricket in Australia too. I understand the problems, the hard bouncing pitches, the blinding light, the heat, the statutory retirement to the beer tent at the end of each six overs. All this can play merry hell with your batsmanship, although the beer tent does not appear to loom so large in the higher grades, and I could see no sign of it at all at the grand Centennial Match. Trays of orange juice strike me as no substitute, but there's always been this yawning abyss between them and us. Sadly the better notions of the village green never permeate to the top, whereas the more unfortunate aspects of behaviour in the first-class game do dribble through to the bottom. Lillee and Thomson, for instance, have sired a whole new generation of rustic body-liners. Not only rustic, I've faced some extremely rude stuff on the roughage of Battersea Park from advertising men and belligerent, beer-soaked cartoonists. I confess that as a captain, my best position, I've frequently called up the

The author strikes a four off Jack Robertson (Middlesex and England) towards the Lord's Tavern, and if you think there is a dash of self-satisfaction in his including such a picture in a sporting tome then you have hit the button in one, brother. I wasn't leaving this one out. With Bill Edrich and Godfrey Evans lurking as well? No way.

quicker bowler to pitch them short, against their better judgement, particularly at public school men, trained to push forward and thus sitting ducks for a short rap on the fingers. They don't like it up 'em. The other unpleasant aspects of the game seeping into the lower reaches are the cheating, as in the great Indian Vaseline Mystery, and what the Australians refer to as 'sledging'.

Now cheating, to coin a phrase, isn't cricket. The fact that if you snick the ball to the wicket-keeper and set off regardless and at once for the pavilion or whatever, you are viewed as a fool and a ninny lowers the tone considerably. If you're out, you should leave. W. G. Grace apparently rarely paid much attention to the umpire, and was given to replacing the bails after being comprehensively bowled, and remarking loudly on the windy nature of the day. Don Bradman would never budge, until the finger had been up for some minutes. Even so, there is a code. I think, however, that anyone is entitled to question an L.B.W. decision. I have never to my certain knowledge been out leg before wicket.

A little gamesmanship can be permissible. *Private Eye* were playing *The Times* a couple of years ago, and *The Times* had introduced a club cricketer of note, in I Zingari hat and Free Foresters sweater, clearly to grind our noses into the dust. He was into his 20s in no

The good Doctor seen in this laughable montage effecting the sort of forward prod you associate with English batsmanship today. The ball passes the bat in Fig. 1 and by Fig. 6 has been returned to the bowler.

time at all and treating our bowling with casual disdain. I was keeping wicket, and grasping at straws, as he let one pass on the off-side, the slips appealed with vigour. 'Not out!' I cried. 'You will note', I said to the umpire at the end of the over, 'that I was not amongst those bothering you with unnecessary questions. *I* only appeal when it's out. Umpiring is no sinecure. We should do all we can to help.' I think he was quite touched. An over later, I organised the slips, clearly this elegant club man with gleaming pads was good for a century or two and we couldn't cope with that sort of target. 'Next time', I said, 'it passes his bat, everybody up. The bowler', I tapped my nose knowingly, 'is already primed'. Next ball it was, our Raffles left it alone with Wooley-like grandeur, and the entire orchestra and chorus raised a 'How was that then?' that caused earth to move near Droitwich, while I held the ball aloft and registered my own plea, both lungs in fourth. Up went the finger and exit left at louring batsman. 'Pick on someone your own size next time', we scoffed. There are, as I said, times when needs must.

I draw the line at 'sledging'. This started as a baseball term. In baseball apparently it is perfectly acceptable for the players to mount the coaching mound and pour the most

THE BATSMAN FROM THE BOWLER'S POINT OF VIEW.

appalling insults and vilifications upon the opposition. Quite often, this ends in fisticuffs, but that is baseball, and there it is and none the worse for that. They *are* foreign, a point people frequently miss when contemplating Americans. Alas, this has now permeated the cricket field, and it is, one gathers, quite acceptable for the close fielders and the wicketkeeper to pour scorn on the batsman in the foulest of language. There's also a deal too much gesturing and histrionics. I have no objection whatsoever to footballers hugging and caressing after scoring a goal, it shows they care, in many cases it is the only evidence of this, you frequently get the impression that their minds are more occupied with their shirt emporiums

Nauseous stoat! Dung-beetle!

You swine, you bounder, you unmitigated rogue!

Bastard!

Practitioner of unnatural vice! Bluebeard! Terror of the Vestry!

Rotter! Bounder! Foreign Cad!

Sledging – the scene of belligerent banter from the close fielders that greets the incoming batsman.

A source of inspiration to any cricketer. 1966 bowling at Aldworth and getting nowhere. (From l. to r. George, Charlie, Frank, the author, Kenneth Cope.)

or hairdressing salons than the game in hand or the side they're playing for. It may not be the side they were playing for last week anyway, loyalty must be hard to come by, and footballers by the very nature of football, a mixture of the slave trade and Hollywood in the thirties, breeds mercenaries. Not so cricket, and anyway it's played in long trousers at the time of writing, and what we need is a little more of what Jack Fingleton has referred to as 'the old charm, the grace and gentility'.

Of course, you can still chat up the batsman. I remember impressing dour, northern cricket-writer Michael Parkinson with a little touch of southern *savoir-faire.* A side I'd raised was playing against the charming village of Aldworth in Berkshire on their pretty ground surrounded by three rows of elm. For some reason I was an hour late and when I arrived Parkinson, who had taken up the reins of office in my absence, had let the game already slip sadly away. The village was 120-odd for no wicket, and Charlie, their bold, bald opener, I gathered from the score-book, was on 94. I was on the pitch in an instant, and realised at once that Charlie had no idea his century was in the offing. 'What a famous way to go to a 100, Charlie', I cried, 'with a mighty sixer'. I could see the lust gleam in his eye. 'Toss one up, Parky', I murmured, 'and he's yours'. And he was, gone with one wild heave and the clack of falling wickets. 'You're a bit of a bastard', said Parky, which I took as something of a compliment. 'It's our ruthless southern ways you'll never get used to', I said.

He is, of course, from Yorkshire, where cricket is a serious business, and indeed it's one of the few counties I would leave intact under my massive plans for revitalising the Championship. It was after all won in 1976 by Middlesex which no longer exists, except as a euphemism for Gay Liberation. Apart from Yorkshire, who live in the past where cricket properly belongs, most of the players who play for counties weren't born there anyway. Some have come thousands of miles to be with us tonight. In my view the tactics of *Come Dancing* should be adopted and more representative areas with wider representation created, such as the North-West and Home Counties (South). Fewer fixtures lasting four days might lure a larger congregation. The popularity of the one-day game is that the spectator can see the whole business in a sitting and a result is guaranteed. The popularity of Test Matches is that sides of greater talent are pitted against each other over five days thus allowing ample time for the necessary fluctuations of fortune that are cricket. My scheme provides for the larger super league matches on Wednesday, Thursday, Friday and Saturday with Sunday and Monday or Tuesday for the one-day contests. It's the sort of British compromise that made us what we were and might cause a few vital coronaries in the Long Room at Lords. But it

is simply this, that I'm anybody's for a game of cricket, and I haven't been to a county match for years. I am clearly not alone. You would have to keep Yorkshire as Yorkshire though or they'd declare U.D.I. and Michael Parkinson would have nothing to write home about.

Nowadays, given the new violence on the village verdure and fear of death in Battersea Park I only play in charity matches. They're friendlier. Also how else would I have played at Lords and Trent Bridge, batted with heroes Edrich and Compton (wearing incidentally my 25-year-old Denis Compton autographed pads, painted with white emulsion annually and still going strong much to the surprise of the autographer)? How else would a bowler of my calibre have collected such a hat-trick as Charlie Drake, the diminutive funster and 'Scobie' Breasley twice? I also have before me a presentation pack of knives, forks and spoons won at Britain's first three-a-side floodlit cricket competition held at Stockport County Football Ground in pouring rain in late 1976. It was to do with sport for all. Sport for some, I think. It was played on matting with a gleaming white hockey ball. John Taylor, the Welsh bionic forward, Jimmy Ellis of *Z-Cars* and me, as unlikely a winning trio as the Barrymores, Ethel included. We beat John Snow's team in the final, I throw in idly and far from modestly. That John Snow is another hero. There can be no wrong in a fast-bowling poet who can drive the M.C.C. mad.

Where to Play

Chances are if you enjoy a game of cricket, you've found a team to play with locally or a touring side to travel with. If not, find 10 others and put an ad in *The Times* or *The Cricketer* asking for opposition. Most sides have holes to be filled in their fixture lists. A number of them have holes to be filled in in their pitches, but the cricket field is invariably the prettiest part of town. Many is the time I've stood at deep fine leg 'twixt thistle and cowpat lost in the beauties of the English countryside, and at the same time, thinking if the *Marylebone* Cricket Club can tour the West Indies, why can't I? Or 'why can't *we*?' to be more accurate, as you'll need help.

Think big, that's the answer. For example, there's a pub side in London, the Phene Philanderers, a lively cross-section of advertising men, writers, inebriates and layabouts, who have in their time toured Paris, Hong Kong, Bangkok, Amsterdam and play annually in Corfu. Greek cricket, yet. A permanent member of my Dot-cricket side when young was X. Balaskas, Xenephon to his friends, a Greek-born leg-break and googly bowler who

played for South Africa in the 1930s. Although I've always known cricket existed on Corfu, I'd always imagined that it was played by British expatriates. In fact, the Corfiots have played cricket since the Napoleonic Wars, learning it from watching the British army and navy at play.

The ground is magnificent. It's in Corfu Town's Spionada Square. One side of the ground is a Rue de Rivoli-like parade of bars and cafés, one of which serves as a pavilion. Opposite stands the old Fort and the former Royal Palace dominates the Harbour End. The pitch is rough grass, except where a gravel path crosses it and the wicket is matting. It serves also as the local park so before play can begin, sweet papers, ice cream wrappers and canine offerings have to be removed.

A local rule is that only one ball is allowed per game. The reason is soon clear. The new ball, after a few trips over the gravel path, loses all sense of shine and respectability. Thus, if the Corfiots win the toss, they field enjoying the best of the ball and leaving only a battered relic for the opposition's bowlers. If they lose the toss they announce that a new ball will not be available until their turn to bowl. These tactics are extremely successful and the only solution is to take your own bag of new balls.

The games begin after the siesta and consist of 33 overs a side. The tactics of the 33-over game they also have down to a nicety. The crowds are extremely knowledgeable and voluble and volatile.

The Philanderers go for a fortnight, with their womenfolk, who for once have no cause to complain about being dragged about like a cricket-bag, and they play the Britannia Club, local British residents as the name suggests and Corfu's two sides, Byron (named after another cricketing poet) and Gymnasticos.

Some Useful Greek Cricketing Terms

Fermadoros *Wicket-keeper*
Bombada *A full toss*
Pintz *A yorker*
Primo slaco *Long hop*
Apo psila *Caught*
Apo xyla *Bowled*
Psili tis gris *A bumper*
Sotto *Out*
Blotto *Been in the pavilion too long under the influence of ouzo*
Owdat? *Howzat?*

There appears to be no word for 'not out' as the cry of 'Owdat?' automatically causes a Corfiot umpire to up the finger.

Noel Baptiste, having organised the Philanderers' tours over the years, has now set up *International Cricket Holidays, 24a Oakley Gardens, London SW3 5QG.* They'll organise tours for your team to Paris, Rome, Lisbon or for the more ambitious, Barbados, Bangkok, Sri Lanka and, of course, Corfu. They reckon five games in a fortnight is sufficient so that it's more of a holiday than a tour. Prices range from £60 for a week in Paris to £497 for a fortnight in Singapore, Penang and Bangkok. I've only ever played them in Battersea Park, but the scheme seems more than sound if your team is fed up with the same old fixtures and has a taste for something more heady than the local Maltdrain's Mediocre Ales.

Cricket for Ladies

There's not much opportunity for the ladies at present unless they join a club affiliated to the Women's Cricket Association. I only mention this because when you look at some of the riff-raff and wreckage of the male inclination used to make up an eleven, and when you look at the standard of some of our lissom womenfolk, it does border on the narrow-minded. However, inspired perhaps by their finally breaking down the doors of Lords under that Boadicea Rachel Hayhoe-Flint, who at the same time led the English side that won the Ashes (well, not the Ashes, rumour has it they play for Joanna Southcott's Box) mayhap attitudes will change. In the meantime they will have to make do with the Hon. Secretary's thanks for the excellent tea.

There are about 60 clubs affiliated to the W.C.A. and they all provide evenings of nets and coaching. There is also a Cricket Week in August – open to any member over 16, to play, umpire, heckle or whatever. So, come along, Ms., you could tour Australia yet, even if the village side won't call upon you. After all, who invented over-arm bowling, I ask you? (The ball, when bowled under-arm, became enmeshed in their voluminous white frocks.) I'm all for mixed cricket, it would certainly cheer up the changing-rooms, even if you don't like the new chintz curtains.

Women's Cricket Association, 70 Brompton Road, London SW3 1EX.

FOOTBALL

Legend hath it, that Brother Lawrence, during a brisk game of handball in the cloisters prior to vespers, suddenly dropped the ball and kicked it. 'Football!' they cried as one, and Friar Bartholomew, who belonged to a breakaway gang of crypto-Cistercians and had been thinking along these lines, indeed he'd already illuminated a rude offside law, suddenly realised that he was on to something vast financially.

'We shall build enormous stadiums, fill them with 10 or 20,000 screaming fans – '

Brother Lawrence began to ink a large sign at once saying 'No Trappists'.

'And', continued the breathless Friar, 'we shall immediately take out vows of covetousness, exploitationness, sheer naked greediness – '

'And lechery?' mooted Brother Lawrence, enjoying a vicious cuff from Friar Bartholomew and incidentally coming up with another pastime.

'We could buy and sell people', said the Friar, 'my word, the permutations are endless'.

Since those dear, dead days the national game has gone steadily downhill, until nowadays it's high time we came up with another. Tenders should be asked for from the monasteries. The Americans are eager to buy up the dusty remains of English soccer, we could let the Arabs have the rest.

We used to be terribly good at it once, we played blunt, forthright football with speedy wingers and whacking great centre-forwards, backs who could tackle, bold goalies who played on with broken necks, and the shorts were longer. But alas since then we have become so increasingly bogged down with technique and technicalities, maps, plans and dossiers, quizzes and probes, theodolites and stopwatches, that what was once an enjoyable bang is now the Kinsey Report. It can't help that the majority of our football grounds have all the attractions of a motorway café taken over by the NAAFI in a military coup. They are gloomy, scruffy places. I can never understand why, when England plays at home, they play at Wembley which is to all intents and purposes, away.

Take a look at the Tampa Bay Rowdies, who operate in Florida under the aegis of T. Beauclere Rogers IV, as if III weren't enough. But, give him his due, three years ago soccer was unknown in Tampa. What he's concentrated on are heavy public relations and the kids. For the kids there are tie-ups with hamburger emporiums, free kazoos so that everyone can join in the Rowdies March at half-time and a summer camp, happily known as Camp Kikinthagrass. A youth league was started with 300 kids and there are now 7000 or more playing. All that, and massive coverage in the press and on television, advertising the game as ideal for the family audience, bags of bands and ballyhoo, leggy cheer-

leaders and the team arriving on the field in fire engines or Zeppelins. At the moment they are buying attractive players, Pele, now retired, George Best and Rodney Marsh, etc., but they hope soon the youth league will start coughing up likely all-American boys. The problem now is to suggest *that* to the Board of Thursday United without being drowned in waves of froth and bile. It all strikes me as making excellent sense, but alas we are not in the hands of the Tampa Bay Rowdies but the Boston Stranglers. The crowds there are apparently happy, and hooligananism hasn't caught on at all. One minor confusion is that, when the game is televised, there must be commercial breaks, so the referee is wired for sound and on a 'bleep' from the producer instantly blows whistle and waves yellow card

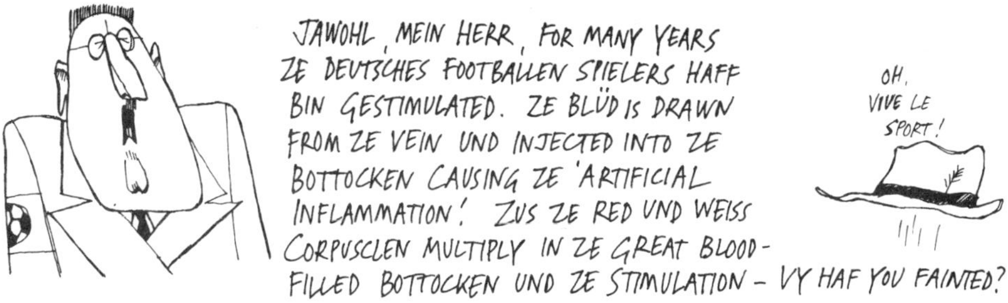

Proof positive that I once kept goal in a football side in 1953 that won a very small cup. This makes me an expert. I have been to Hong Kong three times; this makes me an expert also on the Far East.

The Sauds are playing towards Mecca. In both halves of the game. They insist on this traditionally and, after all, it's their ball.

or calls on the trainer for something from his bucket, so that cheese may be sold for a minute or two.

In the other emergent footballing nation, Saudi Arabia, where the government has put aside £25,000,000 to promote the game and raise a national side, to which end they have hired the services of Jimmy Hill and Bill McGarry, the crowds are equally content. Balloons and drum-beating are extremely popular, and they have been known to release flights of pigeons painted in the black and yellow colours of the home team. Despite the lurking £25,000,000 all the players are unpaid amateurs, and there is no way they'll lure our lads off like the Americans, as the order of the day is 'no alcohol and no women', the life-blood of English football.

If you want a game of football, they're easily found. I play once every seven years, in fact I think I've hung my boots up for ever now. Always leave shouting for 'less'. I retired once having saved a penalty and then scored one in the same minute. The run up the field did for me entirely.

I returned seven years later to play for *Private Eye* against *Time Out* near the Zoo. Taking my own advice, I hid at number nine, and scored a hat-trick, by the simple device of kicking the ball goalwards whenever it came near me. This unsophisticated technique seemed to surprise the opposition, there was even the mild suggestion that it wasn't football.

This being over half-time in the book, here is a story for children. A cautionary tale entirely wasted on you, if you're a leg-biter.

THE POOL THAT MAKES...

£½ Millionaires

6 DIVIDENDS 8 SELECTIONS · MARK X

NOTE REF. No.

TREBLE CHANCE 4 DRAWS 8 RESULTS 4 AWAYS EASIER 6

Home	Away	No.
Q.P.R.	Wolves	1
Stoke	Chelsea	2
Tottenham	Luton	3
Blackpool	Portsmouth	4
Bolton	York	5
Bristol R.	Nott'm F.	6
Norwich	Orient	7
Notts C.	Bristol C.	8
Oldham	Cardiff	9
Sheff. Wed.	Aston Villa	10
South'pton.	Man. Utd.	11
Sunderland	Hull	12
West Brom.	Millwall	13
Aldershot	Peterboro	14
Blackburn	Walsall	15
Brighton	Gillingham	16
Charlton	Bourn'm'th	17
Crystal P.	Port Vale	18
Grimsby	Preston	19
Hereford	Southend	20
Plymouth	Bury	21
Swindon	Hudd'field	22
Watford	Chest'field	23
Barnsley	Reading	24
Camb'ge U.	Crewe	25
Chester	Exeter	26
Doncaster	Workington	27
Lincoln	Darlington	28
Mansfield	Hartlepool	29
Newport	Rochdale	30
Rotherham	Scunthorpe	31
Shrewsbury	Bradford C.	32
Swansea	North'pton	33
Torquay	Brentford	34
Barnet	Tonbridge	35
Chelmsford	Atherstone	36
Dartford	Wealdstone	37
Margate	Guildford	38
Stourbridge	Dover	39
Yeovil	Maidstone	40
Bangor	Boston U.	41
Barrow	Macclesf'ld	42
Netherf'ld	Skelm'sdale	43
Ayr	Hibernian	44
Dundee U.	Rangers	45
Alloa	Berwick	46
Brechin	Raith	47
Cowdenb'th	Clydebank	48
East Fife	Montrose	49
Falkirk	Stranraer	50
Hamilton	Queens P.	51
Meadowb'k	Forfar	52
Q. of South	Stirling A.	53
St. Mirren	Albion R.	54
Stenh'muir	E. Stirling	55

Score-Draw (1-1, 2-2 etc) . 3 pts
No-Score Draw (0-0) . . . . . 2 pts
Away, Void or Postponed . 1½ pts
Home . . . . 1 pt

RESULTS

35

A permutation guaranteed to bring a flush to the cheek of any pools promoter. There is no danger of your following in the steps of Mrs Vivien (Spend! Spend! Spend!) Nicholson with this one. Relax, and read it out loud as you listen to results.

FLÜT v. ENGLAND

OUR GAME IS KICKFISH - KICKING GIANT SQUID WITH FLIPPERS INTO FISH-NETS UNDER-WATER.
LAW

THAT'S QUITE LIKE FOOTBALL, DEAREST
FOOT BALL
LAW

IS FOOTBALL PLAYED WITH SQUID UNDERWATER ?
NO, DEAR, ON GRASS WITH A BALL

THAT IS MUCH EASIER! WE SHALL UNDOUBTEDLY WIN. THE TEAM MUST BE RE-FLIPPERED
MY HERO!

WHAT, ARCHBISHOP, OF THE PITCH ?
AS PER THE ENCYCLOPAEDIA SIRE

PAINTED THIS MORNING, SIRE, BY THE MASTER OF THE DOGS!
MY MASTER-PIECE

PERFECT IN EVERY DETAIL

ONE SNAG!
WHAT ?

IT'S MEANT TO BE FLAT!

IT IS FLAT! THE ARCHBISHOP ROLLED IT PERSONALLY.
IT'S NOT MEANT TO BE AT AN ANGLE OF 75°, MY DUCK

FLÜT IS NOT FLAT. IT'S FAMED FOR BEING NOT AT ALL FLAT. IT IS STEEP. IT IS EXTREMELY STEEP!
FOOTBALL PITCHES ARE FLAT, DEAR

BUT WHERE, SIRE, HAVE WE A LARGE, FLAT AREA SUITABLE FOR FOOTBALL?
I HAVE A NOTION

FLÜTBALL
a new series
FTV

WHERE IS THE GAME TO BE PLAYED, SIRE, CUT TO CAMERA 2!
I TOLD Mr. REVIE THE VENUE

THE GREAT BANQUETING HALL. HE WAS A TRIFLE SHAKEN HE SAID THEY'VE SPORTED ON ALL SORTS OF PITCH – BUT –

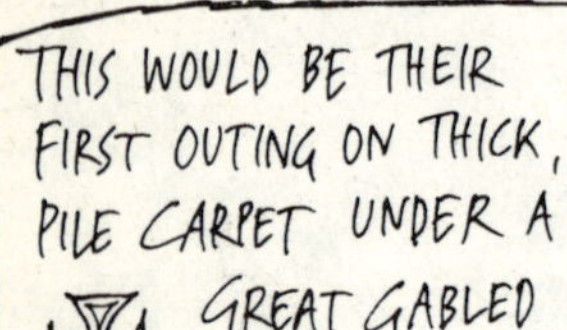

THIS WOULD BE THEIR FIRST OUTING ON THICK, PILE CARPET UNDER A GREAT GABLED CEILING THICK WITH CHANDELIERS.

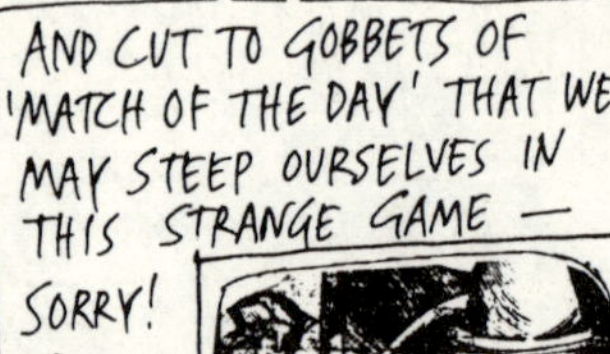
AND CUT TO GOBBETS OF 'MATCH OF THE DAY' THAT WE MAY STEEP OURSELVES IN THIS STRANGE GAME — SORRY!

THEY LOOK VERY GOOD

THIS IS THE WORLD CUP FINAL OF 1966, O ENORMITY

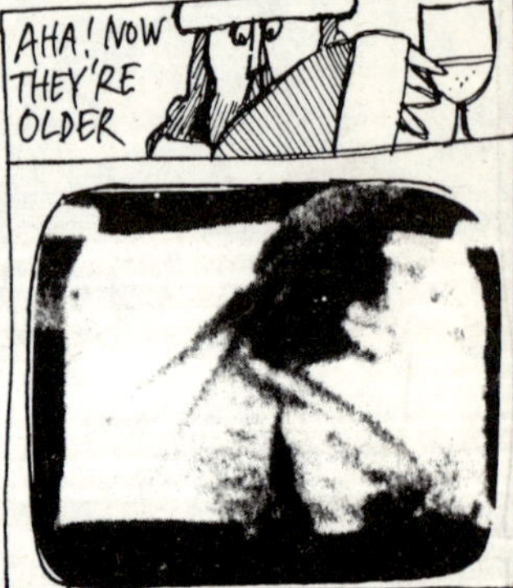
AHA! NOW THEY'RE OLDER

AND NONE THE WISER!

AND DOUBTLESS, SIRE, NOT NEARLY SO SPRY

I THINK I'M GETTING THE MEASURE OF THIS FOOTBALL

THE NIGHT OF THE MATCH. THE GREAT BANQUETING HALL GOES POTTY AS ENGLAND RUN ONTO THE PITCH THROUGH THE DOOR FROM THE GREAT SCULLERY, LEAPING OVER SOFAS AS THEY GO.
The Archbishop BITES YER KNEES
THE GERANIUM ROOLS OK?
What is this Feetbowl? I ask you
HONK FOR FLÜT
CHAMPIONS
ROOT FOR FLÜT!
I SHALL PRESENT YOU TO THE LOBELIA
A PREZZY?
HAMBURG PAID £500,000 FOR HIM
HOW DEAR
YOU'VE NEVER BOUGHT ME ONE!
REMEMBER 'MATCH OF THE DAY', ARCHBISHOP
ARE VE READY?
PEEP
GIRD ON YOUR FLIPPERS
AND CRISPIN CRISPIAN SHALL NE'ER GO BY FROM THIS DAY TO THE ENDING OF THE WORLD BUT WE IN IT SHALL BE
etc.

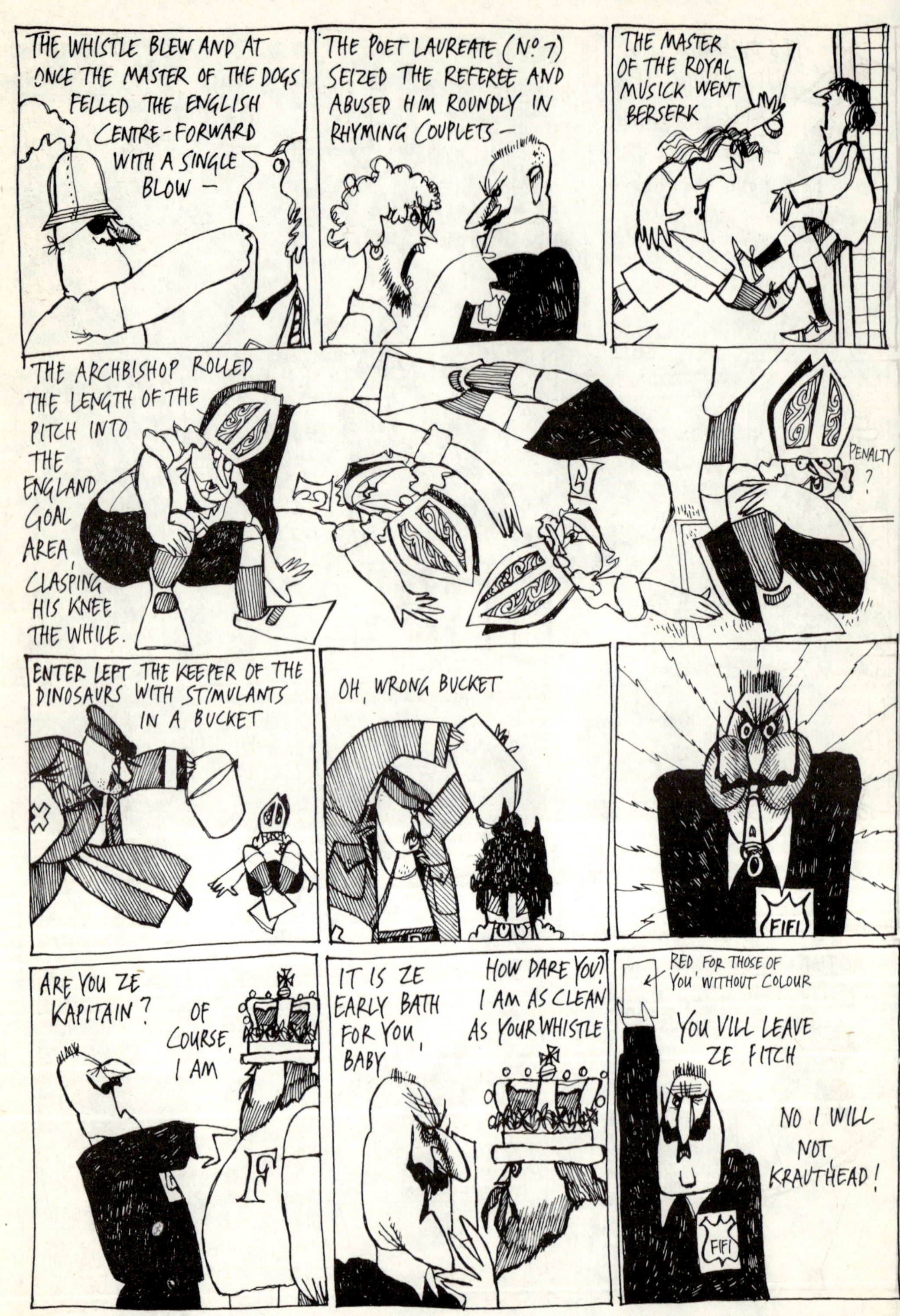
THE WHISTLE BLEW AND AT ONCE THE MASTER OF THE DOGS FELLED THE ENGLISH CENTRE-FORWARD WITH A SINGLE BLOW –
THE POET LAUREATE (Nº 7) SEIZED THE REFEREE AND ABUSED HIM ROUNDLY IN RHYMING COUPLETS –
THE MASTER OF THE ROYAL MUSICK WENT BERSERK
THE ARCHBISHOP ROLLED THE LENGTH OF THE PITCH INTO THE ENGLAND GOAL AREA, CLASPING HIS KNEE THE WHILE.
PENALTY ?
ENTER LEPT THE KEEPER OF THE DINOSAURS WITH STIMULANTS IN A BUCKET
OH, WRONG BUCKET
FIFI
ARE YOU ZE KAPITAIN ?
OF COURSE, I AM
F
IT IS ZE EARLY BATH FOR YOU, BABY
HOW DARE YOU? I AM AS CLEAN AS YOUR WHISTLE
RED FOR THOSE OF YOU WITHOUT COLOUR
YOU VILL LEAVE ZE FITCH
NO I WILL NOT KRAUTHEAD !
FIFI

IT'S MY PITCH. I'M NOT LEAVING IT. I RULE IT. I AM GERANIUM OF IT. I AM THE MONARCH OF ALL I SURVEY AND THAT INCLUDES THIS PITCH
HERE, HERE, YOUR ENORMITY!
HEAR, HEAR, ISN'T IT?
ZE WHOLE TEAM IS OFF! TAKE A CARD
FIFI
WE KNOW THE LAWS, UMPIRE. WE'VE SEEN 27 MATCHES OF THE DAY. WE HAVE DONE NAUGHT UNETHICAL
I VEEP
WE SHALL NOT BE MOVED
EVERYONE'S LEFT, SIRE
THEN WE MIGHT AS WELL PUT THE FURNITURE BACK
WHAT A FAMOUS MATCH, EH? I ENJOYED FOOTBALL. I'M NOT AT ALL EXHAUSTED
WE WERE ONLY ON THE PITCH FOR ONE MINUTE
BUT THEN AGAIN – WHAT A MINUTE!
ACTION-PACKED, WASN'T IT? THE FANS LIKED IT. IT WAS A CROWD-PLEASER.
THEY AT LEAST BEHAVED, SIRE. THERE WERE NO HOOLIGANS IN THE CROWD!
SHOULD HAVE BEEN, I ADMIT. IT ADDS COLOUR. STILL, WE DID OUR BEST
MORAL – PLAY UP PLAY UP AND PLAY THE MAN

If you send someone off take their name and their address.

RUGBY FOOTBALL

It's ludicrously simple to become inveigled into a game of rugby football. From my own experience all you have to do is wander accidentally into the wrong pub of a Friday or Saturday evening, and if it's the local rugby club's rendezvous, they'll be on you in a second. I was sitting there quite peaceably, I remember, enjoying a pint or two and contemplating tomorrow's Yankee when they pounced. 'Played a bit, I expect', they said, prodding me like a prize sow. 'A bit', I said, with some truth, I've watched more rugby but I've played more soccer, probably the best of both worlds. 'Shade past it now, I expect', one quietly threw into the conversation. The gauntlet was down and I'll never learn. 'You are talking', I lied, 'to one of the finer centres to emerge from the Valleys since the War'. That was the moment to mention the cartilage operation, the tragedy that nipped my career in the bud, but I forgot, and weaved a fanciful basket of falsehoods, based on years as a child watching Newport at the Rodney Parade – Ken Jones and Roy Burnett, who but for Cliff Morgan would have been as famous as Cliff Morgan, but you can only have one stand-off at a time even in Wales, where there seem to be more. They were clearly enthralled, and beer flowed freely and free, so I was happy, indeed, in such a state of euphoria, that when I left I found I'd been signed up to play at centre against the Metropolitan Police 'F' side next day. They shouted after me that they'd pick me up at 10, I was confident they'd no notion where I lived. They knew. The bell woke me at 10, and I hid. They rang and shouted, but there was no way the living legend was going to show his face. I've never been able to go back to that pub either. Indeed, I've been eased out of a few by brutish lock-forwards in cavalry twills and striped cravats for shouting loudly that the only language fit to discuss rugby football in is Welsh.

Funnily enough, my last game was against some Welsh. In 1956 I was obliged with 14 others picked at random from a motley gang of army clerks and drivers, to volunteer to play for Divisional Headquarters, Britain's own Foreign Legion, a group of hard-cases and recalcitrants housed between a Germany brewery and a cigar factory. The opposition transpired to be the Welsh Guards, something else entirely; we were quite pleased only to lose by 90-odd points, though they admitted to letting up in the second half. It was without doubt the most awful afternoon ever, but the piss up afterwards was memorable. That is the essence of rugby football. It is for the hearty and extraordinarily hale. Men whose I.Q.s range from super-Mensa to permanently subtable can team up happily for an afternoon and then be rendered wholly equal in the eyes of God by 17 or 18 pints afterwards.

(MEN OF HARLECH)
PLAYING VERSUS ABERTILLERY
DO NOT CALL THEIR LOCK A FAIRY
AND IT'S WISE TO BE AS CHARY
PLAYING VERSUS NEATH
PLAYING AGAINST LLANELLY
YOU SUDDENLY FEEL DEATHLY
YACKY DA
YOUR KNACKERS ARE
OVER THE HILLS AND FAR FROM HEALTHY
IT SEEMS LESS HARD IF
PLAYING CARDIFF
THEY ALWAYS SEND A WREATH
HIS MAX'S BOYCE
There'll be a Welcome in the Hillsides
There'll be a Welcome in the Bar,
There'll be a Doctor in attendance
Should you Collide with J.P.R.
NOW YOU'RE HEADING HOSPITAL BEDWARDS,
THOUGHT YOU COULD GET PAST GARETH EDWARDS
HELLO, SAILOR, CHRIST, IT'S JOHN TAYLOR!

HIDING PLACES FOR THE INEPT

You may yet at some time be inveigled into a ball-game, and apart from advising you to study Stephen Potter, still apposite to this day, I can only suggest the best places to hide on the playing field.

Soccer
Take the Number 9 shirt, the old-fashioned centre-forward. You can make perilous mistakes in defence, and be a constant butt. At Number 9 you can walk up and down the middle of the pitch. To stay on-side simply quicken your step if you see there's only the goalkeeper between you and their goal, there should be one other. Occasionally run away if the ball comes near you, you are making space, this is quite acceptable. The chances of a ball reaching a centre-forward are at best remote, at any level of the game.

Rugby
There are those who will advise you to play among the forwards, that you can lose yourself in the scrum. This is rubbish, nobody is forced to work harder, to run further than a forward. You spend the entire game running the length of the field in order to pack down or take part in a line-out, while everyone else waits impatiently. The wing isn't bad but if you do get the ball, you are expected to run with it very quickly and there's no one to offload it on. You are the last in the chain. Centre three-quarter is the place. Make some frenzied dives well away from the feet of others, and if you get the ball, throw it away at once, backwards. Else, it's quite relaxing and far from energetic.

Cricket
Refuse to bowl, say you're no batsman, but used to keep wicket for Middlesex II until you realised it was too risky for a surgeon's hands. The only embarrassment now can be when fielding. In very low grade cricket, field at mid-off. The off-drive is a thing of the past. A disadvantage, however, is that people will constantly throw the ball to you on its way back to the bowler. In the main, and this applies to any level in which you're obliged to make up the numbers, hide at First Slip. Shout 'Yours!' if the ball comes at you, otherwise jump behind the wicket-keeper, arms outstretched. There is no shame attached to dropping a slip-catch. Everybody does it.

Tennis
This is quite easily avoided. A ricked ankle, a bad back, a Tennis Arse, a Tennis Elbow, are all acceptable excuses for non-participation from Wimbledon downwards. If forced on to a court, commit temporary Hari-Kari or Freddi-Perri (as it's known on court) by serving into the top of your head.

Never be beguiled by the seeming affability or sociability of those who press you to take part in any of those sports. Blood flows just as easily in a 'friendly', particularly after lunch.

To soften the blow in this section (speaking of which, the one essential in cricket even if it's played with a tennis ball against a team of women, is an abdominal protector or box) we shall start with the less painful ball games. I lie.

GAMES TO KILL Other People

By this title I don't mean that killing is the actual purpose of the game, but it used to be. They are sports that erupted basically from man's inhumanity to man. You may prefer those that emanated from the monastic cloisters (with the exception of the Brothers of the Order of St Karate who can halve the Bible with the back of their hands) but these sports evolved as man became more and more adept at wiping out his fellow. I'm surprised we don't have Olympic Grenade-Throwing and International Dam-Busting.

FENCING

In fact, the disappointment of fencing as a sport as far as I'm concerned is that it smacks not a jot of that classic encounter between Errol Flynn and almost anybody, but particularly with Basil Rathbone in that grand old *Robin Hood.* Up and down the staircase of Nottingham Castle they went, employing not only the sword, but cloaks, daggers, tables and Liberace-size candelabra. Now there was a crowd-pleaser, and I for one am all for the introduction of Olympic free-style fencing in which participants are allowed to pre-select certain items of furniture to add to their armoury.

That, alas, will doubtless never be, and in the meantime, in between-time, what we have got if not fun for the casual viewer, is a sport we used to rank high in the world at, but seem to have dropped off sharply in. The reason for this seems to be that whereas we cosset our fencing young with love and money from age six to 20, after that they're on their own. Junior fencers get plenty of coaching and opportunities to compete abroad. We have at the moment the World Youth Champion, Robert Bruniges, a one-handed fencer from Catford. This is all achieved, or certainly the major part of it, by funds raised by the Junior Committee which was started by a band of parents. At 20, this all stops, and suddenly in order to get to the necessary competition, fencers have to dig deep into the pockets of their elegant plus-twos in order to raise their own expenses. There is very little support for the seniors and this is reflected in our lack of success.

There are currently 96 juniors in London under instruction from four professional masters, and if they fail to turn up, they're out. This may seem hard, but gone are the days when public-school trained dilettantes casually flicked the buttons off sweaty foreigners, reducing them to their knees, their waxed moustachios molten and awry, thus picking up idly another medal for the Land of Hope and Glory as was. We now live in constant fear of being cut to pieces like sliced bread by the heavy brigades from Eastern Europe.

The price of your kit depends on whether you work off electricity or not. The cheapest weapon is the foil and, if you elect not to be wired up, you can be fully kitted out for under £30. If however you wish to light up, buzz and whirr with the best of them you could spend £60. The *Amateur Fencing Association, 83 Perham Road, West Kensington, London W14 9SP* will give information required. Subscriptions quite often include tuition as at the London Fencing Club who have an annual sub of £25, which includes three lessons a week.

Strong knees are advisable and a fair degree of fitness and agility. The nature of the sport suggests that you could well end up with one arm and one leg several sizes larger than the rest.

Given that you have the necessary knees, however, there seems to be no age limit. You

can start at six and we heard of a splendid old gentleman, now 88, who competed in the 1912 Olympics and is still taking lessons.

Phencing fraseology

The language is rich and worth bandying about. A *balestra* for instance is a suitable balletic term for a short jump forward from the soles of both feet, usually an elegant prelude to a lunge.

A *barrage* is a tie or fight-off.

A *coquille* has nothing to do with St Jacques, but is the heel-shaped guard of an *epée* or foil.

A *flèche* is a running attack, depending on speed and surprise and not to be confused with a flesh-wound, which is something you shrug off stoically when for instance your head has just been removed by a cannon-ball in the best of the *Boy's Own Paper*.

'On guard!' It's heartening to know that they actually say this, it wouldn't be the same without it somehow.

Parry A defensive action as its name suggests.

Prise de fer is a special movement, preparatory to an attack.

Riposte is your lightning repartee made after a successful parry.

Piste – not an example of your lightning repartee (indeed sobriety would appear to be a must in fencing), but the spot where it's all at.

SHOOTING

In Abu Dhabi, said he knowledgeably, there is a bird known as the Houbara bustard, a succulent bird, he quotes, much enjoyed by local gourmets, among whom one should list the Sheik Zaid, whose hunting hawks kill off a

good 2000 of the miserable bustards a year. Indeed, so rare is the Houbara bustard now in Abu Dhabi, a fact that doesn't go unmentioned in the Abu Dhabi and Joan clubs, that the Sheik and his hawks have to fly by personal VC10 to Pakistan for their bustard-bashing.

The bustard has two things working for it. One, it runs as fast as it flies and secondly, it evacuates its bowels into the eyes of its adversaries thus blinding them. I throw this choice information in for any grouse who may be browsing through these pages. To any other of our feathered friends, perched perhaps on the shoulder of our gentle reader, I offer this further word, it also applies to hang gliders and parachutists, never fly over Italy, where they shoot anything that moves upon the wing.

Shooting has much in common with fox hunting, the same sort of people do it for one, but most obvious is the literary style to be found in both *The Horse and Hound* and, say, *The Shootist.*

'*To lie atop one's gilly in the pouring rain, feeling the prickle of thick tweed against the knees, the cold, muddy fingers of Mother Earth probing seductively and wetly through the seat of one's trousers, to hear distantly the rattle and clink of the approaching gin-trolley being pushed o'er fern and fen by Purdey, my old retainer, to enjoy a Thermos of good, nourishing horse blanket soup, lovingly made up by the Memsahib from the dogs' breakfast left-overs, is to know that God is in his heaven and the mullard are aloft with Him. Blaze away!*' I use this extract from *Glorious Twelfth Bore* by Major-General Sir Benito Custer-Hitler, without permission.

The only shooting I've ever done, apart from one outing with a sten gun in the Army which I shall recall, is at low flying tin cans with a shot-gun. I was, on this first occasion, required to charge down a 20-yard course firing in single shots and bursts at some cardboard replicas of people, and discovered on slowing to a halt that I had peppered the parts of each with shot, as if decorating them with primitive pubic hair, at which I felt sick as a cat. Shooting tin cans though is a cheap version of clay-pigeon shooting and like that sport should cause no ill-feeling from bird-lovers. Conservationists on the other hand may quibble at a field-full of dead tin cans. The machine propels the can with a .22 blank cartridge and can be obtained from Webley and Scott for £5. If you share my preference for shooting at inanimate objects there are 355 clay-pigeon clubs in Britain and

KING GEORGE AS A GREAT SHOT.

membership is only about £2 a year. The major expense is the weapon which can cost anything from £100 to £8000. The clay-pigeons cost £7.50 per 100 and the cartridges at present 7½p each, so to shoot 100 clays will cost £15, and not last very long either. Try breeding them in a kiln.

Further non-violent use of shooters can be found at pistol clubs, who will provide the headphones and the sort of pistol you could never secrete under an armpit. *The National Rifle Association of Bisley Camp, Brookwood, Woking, Surrey* will point in their own direction of Bisley for that annual contest conducted by the most eccentrically clad persons in the most unlikely positions, all aiming to be the one chaired like Druid of the Year from the range to the nearest bar.

To blast bits off our larger birds is extremely expensive. If, for instance, you feel the itching finger write and having writ then moves you to join a syndicate, which rears about 2500 pheasants per annum, with eight guns, this will cost each gun about £1000 a year before you've started. A rough shoot in the south-east ('rough' means no pheasants guaranteed, you simply blaze away Italian style) could cost about £100 a year for about 400 acres.

The alternative is to infiltrate the ranks of the landed gentry. Thus you may be invited to a shooting party. Unfortunately more and more of those gentry, blessed by their birthright with

land, have realised they can keep the woodworm at bay by organising package deals, guns, Range Rovers, gillies, monarchs of the glen, grouse and well-stocked hampers for visiting Americans and Arabs. With Rent-an-

Earl for instance, for very little extra, you get tea and fancies with the family.

Perhaps I'm squeamish but I could never bring myself to shoot a stag. I can never bring myself to eat whitebait because of the accusing look in those rows of tiny eyes. That and my occasional fliration with reincarnation which, if nothing else, must solve the problem of overcrowding on the Elysian fields, make it difficult for me even to terminate a wasp. Stags are even larger, and safe from me.

I was driving through Scotland a year or two ago with small Toby. The weather was appalling. I'd just remarked that Scotland was Nature's own car-wash, and jotted it down as a possible for a Christmas cracker, when we came upon a series of alarming zig-zag bends the like of which I hadn't seen for 20 miles past. And then a startling notice 'Beware – Sheep'. Toby was a little perplexed by this. 'I thought sheep were nice', he said. 'Sheep are nice', I said, 'in the main, but in the Highlands they turn ugly and jump out at you'. The next sign was an elegant silhouette of the stag at bay. I slowed down, not wishing to lock bumpers with some young buck, eager to make a name for himself by rutting with a Rover or whatever. It's lucky we did, as of a sudden there in the middle of the road was a crouching figure in a deerstalker, not unlike Sherlock Holmes in an investigative posture. I peered out through the flailing wipers for a glimpse perhaps of the League of Red-bearded Gentlemen, I had my membership card with me, or a sound of the heady music of the Speckled Band. What greeted the eye was even more amazing. Tweedy men with shooters crawling across the road, nostrils quivering, obviously in search of prey. 'It'll be roast deer up the Manse tonight', I thought. It took a good 10 minutes for the crawling party to

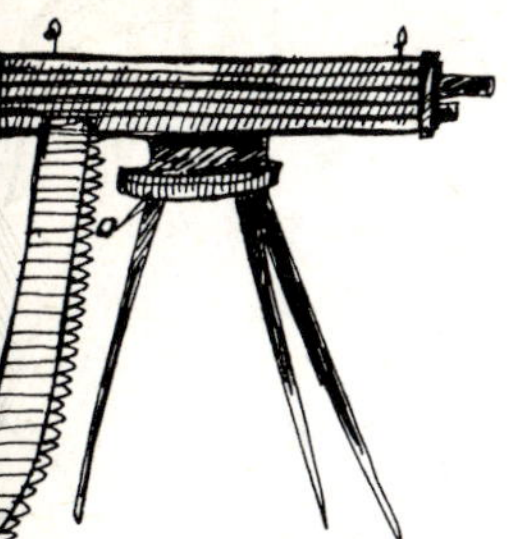

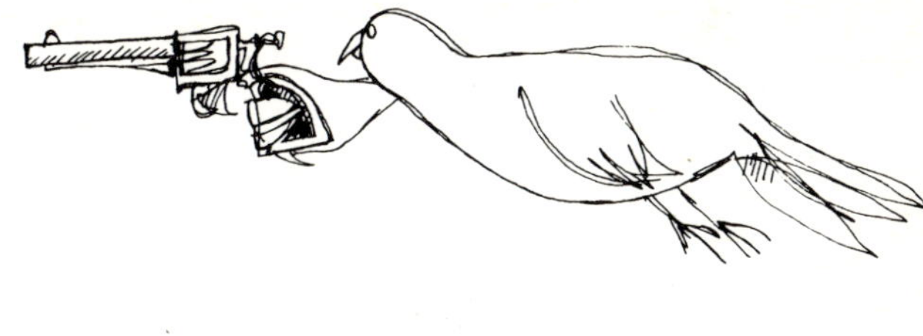

cross. It must be something for the spit they're after, I thought, Mecca is in the other direction. As I began to move slowly forward, I had to brake sharply again, as a flock of gillies paddled across. Some carried decanters and baskets, others had slung between them a rich variety of dead animals and birds. I noticed that many of the more canny wore steel helmets. Several sported artificial limbs.

I wound down the window and spoke to one. An honest-looking fellow in a tartan comforter and bullet-proof vest. He was carrying a mortar.

'What are they after?' I asked.

He pointed up the hill to a herd of Highland cattle. As he did so there was a thunder of shots and high-pitched giggling and the entire cast threw itself as a man into the nearest ditch. I've poked fun at sacred cows, but that was going too far.

Nor could I be a fowler, and be up at dawn in freezing weather crouched in boat or manhole disguised as a tuffet until the duck come in to feed. I'll stick to shooting old duck soup cans.

You will need a gun incidentally, and for that you'll need a licence, whether you intend to fire the gun or not. You can fire one at any age – an alarming thought, but cannot own one until 17 (a shotgun at 15). The police issue gun licences and ask a series of awkward questions about mental disorders, convictions, etc. A shotgun licence is £5, but a Section I Fire Arms Certificate costs £12 a year.

Clay Pigeon Shooting Association, 107 Epping New Road, Buckhurst Hill, Essex.

National Rifle Association, Bisley Camp, Brookwood, Woking, Surrey.

National Small-Bore Rifle Association, Codrington House, 113 Southwark Street, London SE1 0JW.

ARCHERY

I once owned a yew tree from which the bows that won Agincourt were lopped and shaped. In fact it was a slightly younger relative of one that actually was thus employed in the local churchyard. Nonetheless it made one proud. The names still live in telephone directories, Fletcher, Bowman – and millions listen to *The Archers*. Funnily enough, the headmaster of my preparatory school, an establishment straight from *Decline and Fall* with its own built-in Captain Grimes, had been Captain of England at archery in the 1930s, so we were taught the rudiments of the long bow. Extremely satisfying it was too, healthier than darts, and not so fattening.

It's a good sport for beginners as the skills are basically simple, though as you improve and the bows become more complex, it

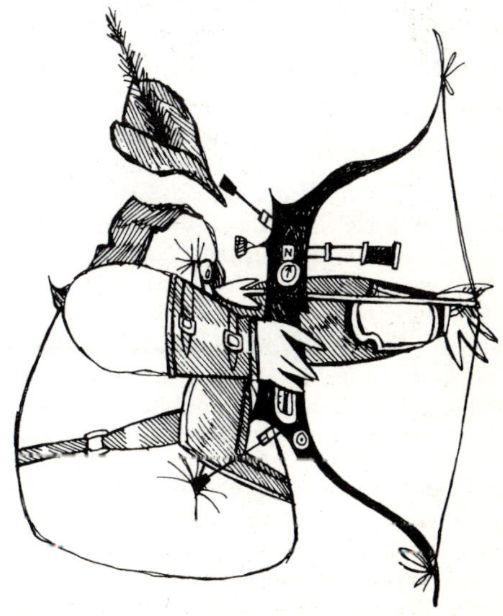

Requiem for a British Heavyweight

becomes progressively more difficult. You don't have to be particularly strong, there's a bow for everybody. There are bows as used in the past by Mongolians which are impossible to bend or shift. You can do it outdoors or indoors, at sports centres, or with clubs or evening classes. Approach the *Grand National Archery Society* (*They* shoot horses? Don't they? Surely not) at the *National Agricultural Centre, Stoneleigh, Kenilworth, Warwickshire.*

Get advice, when buying your first bow, you'll need that, eight arrows and a quiver, a bracer – not a swift gin to cure your quiver but to protect your arm – and a leather glove or tab to guard your hand. This could all come to £50 or £60, but you can do better second-hand. I once saw an advertisement in the *Exchange and Mart* offering a matching pair of artificial legs for an archery kit. There are 1000 clubs in the U.K. and the cost of coaching (£3-£5) is deductable from the first year's sub (£7-£10) if you decide to keep up with it. The clubs are eager for new members and to provide tuition.

There is a branch of the sport based loosely on golf, in which you are let loose in a carefully emptied wood with bows and arrows and fire off at a series of targets from specified spots dotted throughout the course.

The more advanced bows nowadays bear little relation to the old long bow, covered as they are in telescopic sights, computers, range-finders, radar, etc. But we've come a long way since Agincourt, and the bow is still a considerably less offensive weapon than the Armalite rifle, the broken bottle or for that matter the motor bicycle.

BOXING

Muhammed Ali is one of the few who could persuade you that boxing has no effect on you physically or mentally and indeed is of a positive benefit, if not to mankind, then certainly to the bank manager and like hangers-on. On the whole it's not a pretty sight and can lead to mangled brains, eyebrows like Harry Cro-Magnon, or a cauliflower nose for life. If boxing is a skill, which it is, the object being to

pick points off the opponent's target area, then why, you may ask, don't they keep those massive brain-protectors on their heads which they wear for sparring when they step into the ring? The cigar-belching moguls might say that you're unlikely to fill the Madison Square Garden if the heavyweight championship of the world is to be contested between two folk thus attired, suggesting that coursing blood, the ping of teeth being spat into buckets, the swollen heads, the oozing grey cells are all part of the rich pageant, and make it the sport it is. The fact that American footballers wear full armour, and are viewed as none the less butch for that, or that cricketers wear thigh-pads and boxes, makes those sports no less popular. Lillee is quite as dangerous as Ali, and there's nothing more ludicrous than a fight being stopped because two heads have cracked together. What sort of game is that?

It is the only sport in the world in which the insensibility of the one participant is the main purpose of the other. Even in Rugby League they draw the line at that for quite long periods. It strikes me that amateur boxers (the ones in vests) could lead the way on this one.

Good Lord, I was once house captain of boxing, which sounds worth a chapter or two in *Tom Brown's Schooldays* and a deal of adulation from the junior boys. However, I only took on the job on the condition that no one in the house boxed, a revolutionary step in those days. Boxing should be encouraged, they still say, it releases aggressions, breeds self-discipline, strengthens character. My theory was that it hurts quite unnecessarily and

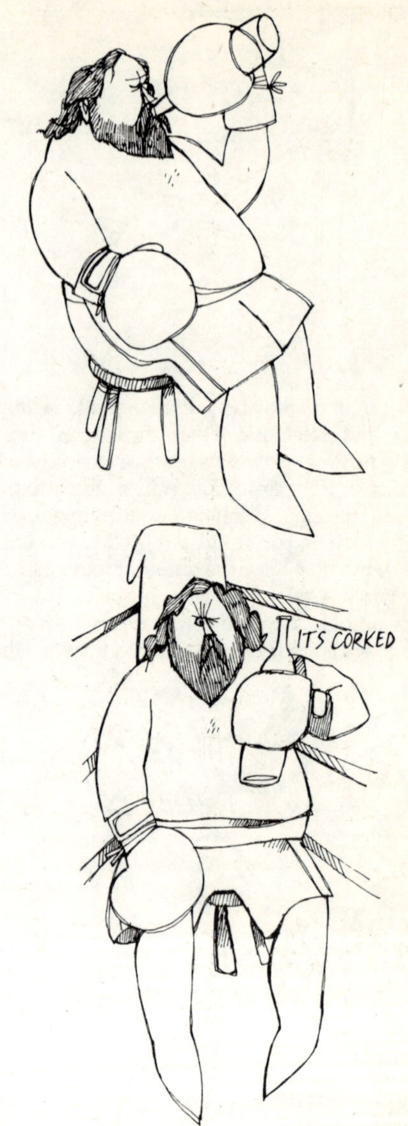

anyway I felt I was striking a blow for Dr Edith Summerskill, a keen opponent of the sport. Name a woman silly enough to box. Quite.

Hypocritical to the last, I thoroughly enjoy watching heavyweights at it, though I haven't much time for the smaller performers or amateurs. But give me a world heavyweight contest and I'll be there like a shot, they seem more able to look after themselves anyway and the ballyhoo is better.

Most boxing is learnt in schools, boys' clubs and Y.M.C.A.s, for the reasons I listed, character-building and the rest. Also the equipment is cheap, and it slows them down. The training is endless, skipping and punching bags, roadrunning and weightlifting. There are admittedly opportunities to travel, but what a way to go.

I would like to put on record that John Conteh and Henry Cooper are two of the most charming souls I know, and wonderful singers. This is in case I meet them again.

Amateur Boxing Association, 70 Brompton Road, London SW3 1EX.

Games
for
SUICIDALS
GOVERNMENT HEALTH WARNING
ON EVERY PACT
TAKE UP
PARACHUTING!
SKY-
PILOTS
HANDBOOK
O.W.P.B.
BUTCHER

I have never found the whiff of danger particularly conducive to sport or relaxation for that matter. *Physical* danger anyway. The musky aroma of Mrs Bradley of course set the pulse racing when young, and I can never pass a fish shop without falling into a fine muck sweat. There are those however who need the hot blast of adrenalin and red lights flashing – men like Irvine who climbed almost to the top of Everest with Mallory, equipped only with a rowing blue. Heroes of the old school, great red-faced men, giants of their time who could only be decently clad by Soft Furnishings. Men who could put down some Tibetan uprising of a morning and still shoot 63 on the Old Royal Lhasa Golf Course prior to tiffin, and died, as many of us would wish to have lived, clinging to the side of Annapurna shouting the complete works of Horace at a startled Sherpa. Men who, had they lived, would have been 100 again next Wednesday. We don't build heroes like that any more. We do little men. In the old days they knew there was only one decent way out for an Englishman. The loaded Luger in the den. Nowadays, one can only recommend the following pastimes and live in hope.

HOT-DOG SKIING

Snow and ice have been known to cause temporary insanity for example Captain Oates, ice hockey players, lunatic American and Canadian skaters who jump barrels (they are still pursuing the elusive 17), and perhaps highest on the list – hot-doggers.

If you have ever felt that the ski-jump is not for you, vertigo perhaps or agoraphobia or a sudden yellow streak, and nothing can put you off your leap more speedily than the sight of nude Japanese bursting from the crowd, then I would suggest you avoid hot-dogging or free-style skiing like the plague.

The hot-dogger usually indulges in aerial acrobatics, whistling down a specially designed ski-jump with a lip at the end that throws him or her high enough in the air to perform different twists and somersaults prior to landing. These suicidal movements rejoice in names like 'back-scratcher', 'daffy', 'helicopter', or 'Moebins flip', which sounds like a disgusting egg nog conceived under laboratory conditions. Alternatively they go for the 'Mogul' event. This is a speed event, with improvised tricks on the way, but basically a race against the clock down a bumpy, virtually vertical snowfield.

The attraction of the sport, apart from its ability to pull crowds of ambulance buffs and vulture fanciers, is the enormous amount of money to be made from prizes and sponsorship. What sponsors and advertisers like about the game is that the slogans and brand-names printed all over the contestant and his hardware are more easily viewed than in the more traditional branches of skiing.

Although at the moment it is American-dominated, mainly because they invented it and it hasn't been around long anyway, Europe may shortly be alive with hot-doggers.

It seems that such are the dangers that insurance cover is becoming prohibitive in the States and they may all be obliged to move in our direction.

Memo to self – take out Insurance against Act of Low-Flying Hot-dogger.

There is a British Freestyle Association which organises competitions in Scotland – weather permitting. Ladies are equally welcome, and indeed equally adept. The 1976 top prize-winner was an American girl. It is good to see that lunacy knows no discrimination.

HANG GLIDING

Hang gliding as a sport ran the gamut in no time whatsoever. In no time at all it was being hailed as a thing of beauty, the television showed the pretty things gliding over England's green and pleasant to the strains of some pastoral piece. Then in next to no time at all there were a number of fatalities and cries from ROSPA and M.P.s for legislation and control. It looked as though the sweet bird of youth was to be caged. As hang gliders rightly pointed out, of course the sport is risky, and relatively pointless if not to some extent risky, but not as risky as made to appear by bird-brained novices who, inspired by the beauty, the pastoral music, the seeming ease of the sport, leapt off cliffs clinging to home-made gliders and failed to understand the sudden proximity of the beach. Like life, it isn't meant to be easy.

Now the British Hang Gliding Association has a code of practice and the more popular spots are carefully watched over by affiliated clubs. There's a full-time Training Officer who patrols the schools seeing that they keep up to

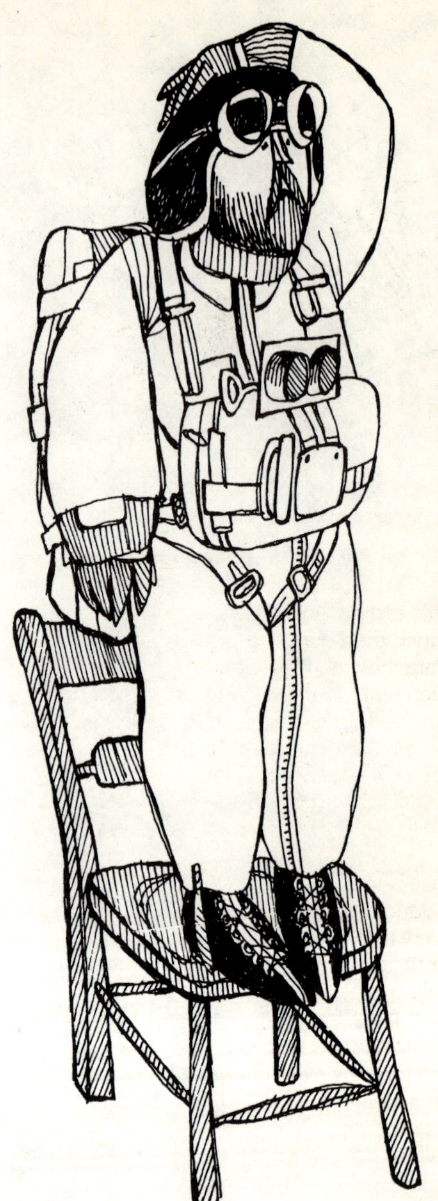

the mark. Most of the trouble and the ugly rumour has spread from inadequate tuition. It's quite a technical business getting aloft and staying there. When hang gliding first spread here from America (NASA had come up with a steerable parachute for capsules returning from Space, but ultimately rejected it) the first fans were pilots, civil and service, and others with some knowledge of aeronautics. A hang glider is, they point out, a flying machine.

Go therefore to one of the many schools, it takes only a few days to achieve competence given proper instruction. Some schools have double-seater gliders which sound the most practical for training-flights. You can hire a kite and get a day's instruction for about £10. This should get you an Elementary Pilot's Certificate, it might take a day or two longer, but it enables you to buy a glider. Second-hand they cost about £100 or £250 and upwards for a new one. Membership of the B.H.G.A. costs £5 and includes third party insurance. Your local club will give you a list of approved sites in the area, and news of any competitions. Quite sensibly, the sites have to be registered (50p a day or so for use of) as farmers can turn ugly should you swoop down uninvited like a wolf on their hysterical fold.

Fitness helps as it is worth remembering that having soared bird-like from the top of the hill, you have to return goat-like to the summit again before further bird impressions.

Incidentally the sport was not unknown in Europe and America in the 1890s, but it was NASA and the telly that caused it to blast off.

The kit, strong ankle-boots with no protrusions, padded and warm clothing, gloves and a crash-helmet – which should only set you back about £8. Chicks away, baby.

British Hang Gliding Association, Monksilver, Taunton, Somerset.

PARACHUTING

When I was in the Army, I was for a while on the permanent staff of the Westminster Dragoons, which sounds as unlikely as it looks. They were Territorials housed in the Horseferry Road and the only moment of discomfort was attending their Annual Camp at Castlemartin, a Welsh beauty spot in Pembrokeshire under martial law. We shared a row of tents

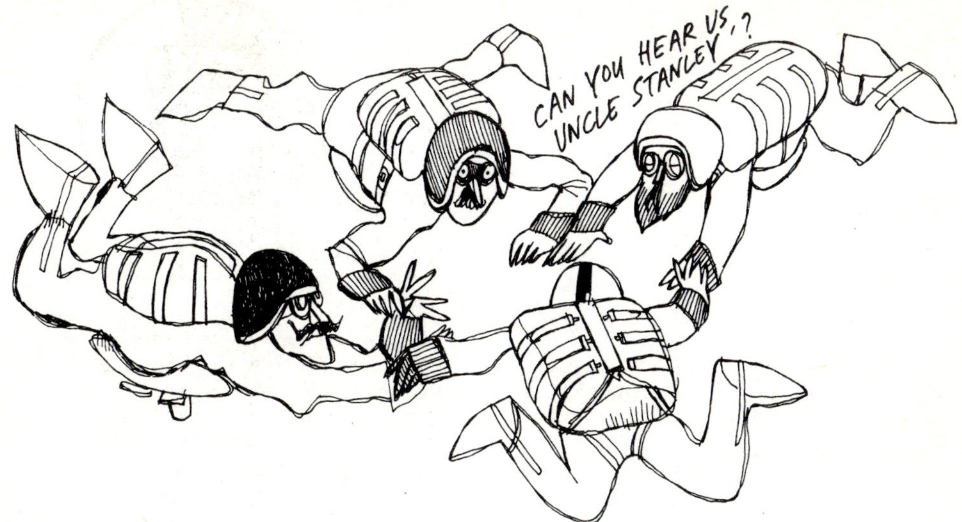

with some paratroopers, an infinitely hardier bunch than our gang of saloon bar cowboys. 'Parachuting', they would say in the NAAFI beer tent, 'is the second greatest thrill in a man's life'. As the greatest thrill was totally unobtainable under canvas in those parts, and even if it was obtained locally would only rate about thirty-eighth in the charts, few argued, but they clearly were wholly hooked.

Before going to parachute school you must have a medical. No diabetics or epileptics for instance, and they frown slightly upon the overweight as the more obese can come to earth too heavily for comfort. Then, if all is well, get provisional membership (£3.71, third party insurance inclusive) of the *British Parachute Association.* Six hours' training and jumping all on the one day will cost £25. After that it costs £2.50 a jump. The second greatest thrill in the world only lasts two and a half minutes, which makes it £1 a minute. This is, of course, still cheaper than the greatest thrill in the world on occasion, but there's less chance of breaking a leg, unless two pages of the *Kama Sutra* stick together and you fall off the wardrobe, essaying the Congress of the Alley-Cat.

The point of parachuting however is that its pleasures never cloy and that as you progress through the various licences, awarded about every hundred jumps, you discover free-falling (120 m.p.h. as opposed to 12 m.p.h.) and the more ambitious techniques of target-jumping. I played in a charity cricket match at R.A.F. Cranwell last year and the tea interval entertainment was a mass-landing on the pitch of the R.A.F.'s Parachuting Display Team, The Falcons. Now you would have thought, despite the 'oohs' and 'ahs' they drew from the crowd as they landed, coloured smoke billowing from their boots, on half a sixpence, standing casually removing their parachutes for the umpteenth time, that they might have professed to slight *ennui.* Not at all, they'd relished every moment. One admitted he couldn't wait to get up again. Exactly like the greatest thrill, you cry, insatiable rogue.

British Parachuting Association, Kimberley House, 47 Vaughan Way, Leicester.

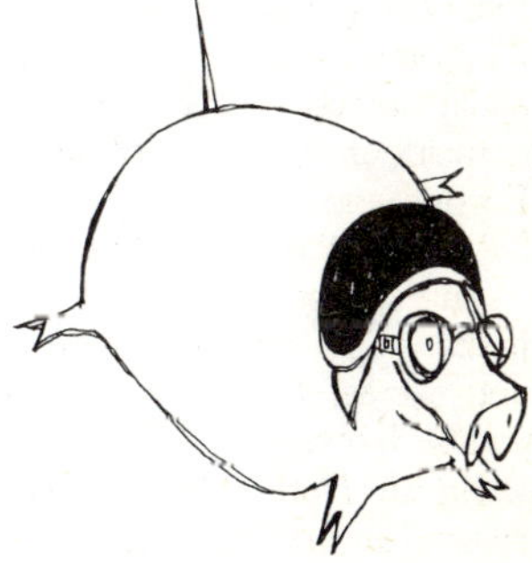

Boomerang Throwing made easy

In the early days the Aboriginals devised two types of boomerangs. The Killer boomerang and the Comeback boomerang.

The Killer made with only a slight curve and much heavier than the Comeback was thrown so that one of its spinning ends would touch the ground to accelerate the spin and thus gather destructive force as it flew into enemy formations.

The Comeback is one the making and throwing of which has been only a pleasant and popular pastime with the aboriginal people.

Some of the tough and beautiful Queensland timbers from which our boomerangs are made include Black Wattle, Ferny leaf Wattle, Brigalow, Lancewood and Ringed Stringybark.

It is imperative to grip and throw all boomerangs so the flat surface begins and flies on the outer side of the circle.

With the body and shoulders held in right direction, lean back drawing hand with boomerang behind the head. Take aim which is 45 deg. into oncoming breeze and approximately 30 deg. upwards and away from the ground.

Lunge forward and throw releasing the boomerang with a whip cracking action imparting plenty of spin.

Most boomerangs are referred to as right handers because they traverse (fly) an anti-clockwise circle, beginning on your right. Some boomerangs are called left handers because they traverse a clockwise circle beginning from your left. Both types can be used for either right or left arm throwing.

CAVING AND POT-HOLING

Perilous pastimes at worst and best. If you pot-hole you go straight down vertically, the aim being to 'bottom' the pot-hole. Caving is the same sort of activity but on the horizontal. The Midlands is the hot-bed of pot-holing.

Years ago when *The Observer* newspaper decided upon a colour magazine, John Wells, *chansonnier* and bon viveur, and I, were asked to provide a weekly piece with pictures. We saw a future full of free trips to the Far East, the West Indies, lightening sketches of the natives and the local Hilton, a few jokes and a deal of food and drink. *The Observer* saw it otherwise and our first piece far from being a racy item on the pleasures of Tonga, was about the litter problem at London's stations. Thinking that in Week Two it might show our versatility if we studied the same problems in Paris, perhaps, we mooted this expectantly, only to be informed that it *was* National Pot-holing Week, they wanted a story and they wanted it quick. News-hungry, professional to our boots, eager to probe and poke, in the highest standards of investigative journalism we bought a book called *Pot-holing* and composed a quick tale thereupon. No one who read it would have doubted for a second that in crash-helmets and boots, with lamps and ladders we had not explored the joys of Boggart's Roaring Hole end to end and bottom to bottom. I don't even know where Boggart's Roaring Hole is, but I like its style.

Nowadays there is an even more sophisticated form than of yore. There are those who set off with aqualungs to swim under the Pennines in pitch darkness, with little idea of direction or distance, and the nagging knowledge that aqualungs don't last forever. Their only companions are blind fish. Claustrophobia looms.

The National Caving Association will put you in touch with fellow-cavers and pot-holers, from their office in the stygian bowels of *3 Greenway, Hulland Ward, Derby DE6 3FE*, and fellows you will need, these are not pastimes to pursue solo.

In America, by the way, cavers are called spelunkers. Perhaps its onomatopoeic.

MODERN PENTATHLON

Given the success of Fox and Co. at Montreal, the sheer likeability of the firm and the obvious enjoyment they displayed, it's not surprising if you contemplate a crack at this *mélange* of five sports. But you'll need to be able to fence, ride, swim, run and pistol-shoot. The fact that Fox and Co. were only given one gold medal between the four of them simply demonstrates the old contention that the camel is not only a horse designed by a committee, but that an Olympic committee – and it's true of almost any sporting body, is a committee drawn up by camels, about to collapse under the terminal straw on the Golden Road to Samarkand.

There are clubs who concentrate on the pentathlon alone, these can be found through the *Modern Pentathlon Association of Great Britain, 1a Godstone Road, Purley, Surrey CR2 2DH.* There aren't that many clubs though and you may have to juggle with a variety of clubs to get your fencing, riding, pistol-shooting, swimming and running. Not to mention juggling with a variety of clubs, a pleasing pastime but not alas included in the pentathlon. At least if you become competent in the five sports, you stand a fair chance of appearing in the musical version of *The Prisoner of Zenda* or 'A Chorus Line of Musketeers'. You might even be hired for that lunatic commercial in which a sporting gentleman clad in black goes through hell and heavy water, the decathlon *in toto*, and is so knackered when he finally makes it to his paramour's bedroom that all he can come up with is a large box of waterlogged chocolates with pathetically soft centres.

You may have to find either a fencing club or one other to start with and then take up the others. Quite often, for instance, there's a pony club that will run a triathlon (running, swimming and riding). You may have to join five different clubs. Despite our success at it, it gets no help as yet from the Sports Council, and the instruction is a trifle haphazard. You may find an instructor who will have you fencing like Errol Flynn and shooting like Wild Bill Hicock, but this is of little use if in the pentathlon you fall off your horse immediately and drown in the water jump.

Anyway the Association will try and point you in the right direction. The kit is a fair outgoing, there being a number of get-ups and implements. In all perhaps as much as £375. A pistol can set you back £250, unless you can get one second-hand. And of course the club subscriptions will vary, depending on how many you have to join. If you do have to join five, it will help fill up the space under your name in *Who's Who*. An evening of fencing can cost you £1.50, not to mention the kit and sub. (*See Fencing*). If, however, the bath cap, the fencing mask, the running shoes, the jodphurs and the holster fit, wear them. When I choose to go, I think the Pentathlon is the decent way out for an English gentleman.

William Rushton's INDEX
Formula Ford 2000 Championship Race

A qualifying round of the Lord's Taverners Formula Ford 2000 Championship.

EVENT 5
15.55 hrs
20 Laps

If the two practice sessions are run in similar conditions this race will comprise the fastest 26 cars from these two sessions. If the two practice sessions are not run undei similar conditions the fastest 13 in each session will make up this race.

Oh AVA, LET
ME TAKE YOU
AWAY FROM THIS
INDEX

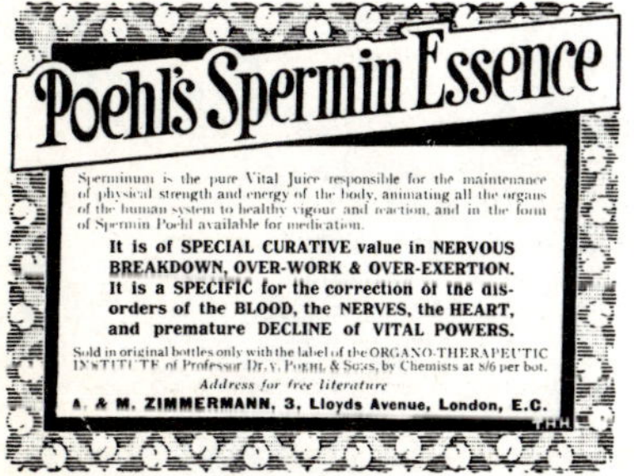
Poehl's Spermin Essence
Sperminum is the pure Vital Juice responsible for the maintenance of physical strength and energy of the body, animating all the organs of the human system to healthy vigour and reaction, and in the form of Spermin Poehl available for medication.
It is of SPECIAL CURATIVE value in NERVOUS BREAKDOWN, OVER-WORK & OVER-EXERTION. It is a SPECIFIC for the correction of the disorders of the BLOOD, the NERVES, the HEART, and premature DECLINE of VITAL POWERS.
Sold in original bottles only with the label of the ORGANO-THERAPEUTIC INSTITUTE of Professor Dr. v. Poehl & Sons, by Chemists at 8/6 per bot.
Address for free literature
A. & M. ZIMMERMANN, 3, Lloyds Avenue, London, E.C.

SOME SPORTING BOOKS

PIGS

PIG-STICKING OR HOG HUNTING	Baden-Powell Bart. Sir Robert	Herbert Jenkins	1924
MODERN PIG-STICKING	A. E. Wardrop	Macmillan	1914

HORSES AND OTHERS

THE HORSEMAN'S COMPANION – A GUIDE TO RIDING AND HORSES	Rayner J. (*Editor*)	Croom Helm Ltd	1974
RIDING FOR PLEASURE AND PROFIT	Stewart K.	Stanley Paul & Co.	1966
BEGINNER'S GUIDE TO PIGEON RACING	Bishop S. W. E.	Pelham	1975
WIN AT GREYHOUND RACING	Clarke H. E.	Stanley Paul & Co.	1974
ENGLISH FOX HUNTING	Carr R.	Weidenfeld & Nicholson	1976
BEAGLERS	Lloyd J. I.	A. & C. Black	1971
BAILY'S HUNTING DIRECTORY		J. A. Allen	Annual

MACHINES

RALLYING	Turner S.	G. T. Soulis	1973

SEA AND SKI

TACKLE WATER SKIING THIS WAY	Briscoe F.	Stanley Paul & Co.	1969
WE LEARNED TO SKI	The Sunday Times	Collins	1975
SURFING IN GREAT BRITAIN	Thomson C.	Constable	1972
SURFING: A MODERN GUIDE	Prytherch R.	Faber and Faber	1972
A BEGINNER'S GUIDE TO CANOEING	Byde A.	Pelham	1973

NO-ONE BUT YOURSELF TO BLAME

WRESTLING	The Training & Education Association		1974
JUDO	Nakabayashi S.	Oaktree Press	1974
TACKLE ATHLETICS	Watts D.	Stanley Paul & Co.	1974
ENJOY YOUR ROCK CLIMBING	Greenback A.	Pelham	1976
THE CHALLENGE OF ORIENTEERING	Pirie G.	Pelham	1968
MATCH SHORE FISHING	Gledhill B.	A. & C. Black	1972
FLY FISHING	Bruce R.	G. Bell & Sons	1963
WHERE TO FISH	Orton D. A. (*Editor*)	Harmsworth	Annual
MODERN SEA ANGLING	Arnold R.	Kaye & Ward	1970
THE COMPLETE GUIDE TO COARSE FISHING	Wrangles A.	David & Charles	1973
TROUT FISHING	Turing H. D.	A. & C. Black	1959
IN PURSUIT OF BIG FISH	Mason M.	Herbert Jenkins	1968
SHARK HUNTER	Housby T.	Priory Press	1976
SHARK ANGLING IN GREAT BRITAIN	Caunter Brig. J. A. L.	George Allen & Unwin	1961
WOODBINE ANGLING YEARBOOK	Colin Graham	Queen Anne Press	1972

BALLS

BEGINNER'S GUIDE TO SQUASH	Hawkey R.	Pelham	1973
YOUNG SPORTSMAN'S GUIDE TO TENNIS	Hull-Jacobs H.	Thomas Nelson & Co.	1961
SNOOKER – HOW TO BECOME A CHAMPION	Williams R.	W. Luscombe	1975
BEGINNER'S GUIDE TO BOWLS	Johnson C.	Pelham	1975
BASKETBALL	Browning W.	Pitman	1964

KILLERS AND SUICIDALS

ALL ABOUT FENCING	Anderson B.	Stanley Paul & Co.	1970
BOXING	Cooper H.	Pelham	1975
SHOT GUN AND SHOOTER	Carlisle G. L. & Stanbury	Barrie & Jenkins	1970
SHOOTING GAME	Kemp M.	A. & C. Black	1972
POT-HOLING	Heap R.	Routledge & Kegan Paul	1964
THE ARCHER'S CRAFT	Hodgkin A. E.	Faber and Faber	1974

ALL SPORTS

ENCYCLOPAEDIA OF SPORT		Marshall Cavendish	1975
RULES OF THE GAME	Diagram Group	Paddington Press	1974

KNOW THE GAME A series of booklets on individual sports published by EP Publishing Ltd.